Girls:
What's So Bad
About Being Good?

Girls: What's So Bad About Being Good?

How to Have Fun, Survive the Preteen Years,
and Remain True to Yourself

Harriet S. Mosatche, Ph.D.
(with Some Help from Her Daughter, Liz Lawner)

THREE RIVERS PRESS
NEW YORK

Published in the United States by Three Rivers Press, an imprint of
the Crown Publishing Group, a division of Random House, Inc.

THREE RIVERS PRESS and the Tugboat design are registered trademarks of Random House, Inc.

Originally published by Prima Publishing, Roseville, California, in 2001.

Interior design by Lori Buley.

Library of Congress Cataloging-in-Publication Data
Mosatche, Harriet S.
Girls: what's so bad about being good : how to have fun, survive the preteen years,
and remain true to yourself / Harriet S. Mosatche
p.   cm.
Includes index.
1. Preteens—Life skills guides. 2. Girls—Life skills guides—Juvenile literature. I. Title.
HQ777.15.M65   2001
646.7'00835—dc21   2001024657

ISBN 0-7615-3289-7

Printed in the United States of America

www.crownpublishing.com

10 9 8 7 6 5 4 3

First Edition

To preteen and teen girls everywhere
who want to have fun and remain true to themselves.

Contents

Chapter Five: Lessons in Learning

Making Your Time Count in and out of School

Chapter Six: Make It Happen in Your Community

Taking Action and Making a Difference

Chapter Seven: Global Citizens

Embracing Diversity and Making Friends Around the World

Chapter Eight: Dream On

Creating—and Managing—Your Future

Acknowledgments

We thank Prima Publishing and the wonderful people who work there—Denise Sternad, Michelle McCormack, and Pat Henshaw—for giving us an opportunity to work on a book together. We also thank Ivan Lawner, loving husband and caring dad, who always willingly left the computer so we could meet yet another deadline, and Rob Lawner, terrific son and supportive brother, who shared his perspective and ideas with us when we asked. We're grateful that both understood how important writing this book was to us.

Introduction

Do you remember being about seven years old and seeing a girl of twelve or thirteen? She seemed so together, so cool . . . so old. Well, now you're that age or close to it. What are you thinking about? Feeling? Looking forward to? Scared about? What questions do you have?

That's where this book comes in. It's your very own personal guide to feeling good about growing up. You'll find out how to:

* Feel good about how you look
* Speak with *confidence* and stay true to the real you
* Feel comfortable with kids you've just met and understand those who live halfway around the world
* Deal with bullies and brats and assorted other difficult people
* Get along with your family (yes, even your little brother) and be a real friend
* Make good things happen in your community
* Challenge yourself to be the best you can be, in school and out
* Dream of a terrific future, and start making it happen!

You may have noticed that I wrote this book with my daughter, Elizabeth (Liz) Lawner. We want you to know who we are, why we decided to work together on this book, and how sharing two different viewpoints will be a plus for you.

Harriet says: Even when I was really young, I knew I wanted to do something to help kids. From the time I started school at the age of five until I graduated from high school at seventeen, my career goal was to become a kindergarten teacher. But while I was in college, I decided to become a psychologist, specializing in child and adolescent development. That meant a lot of years of study, but it's a decision I've never regretted. In my career, I've taught college students about children, and I've taught parents how to understand their kids better. Having worked for Girl Scouts of the USA for many years, I've had the chance to write books for girls and about girls. And I've had lots of opportunities to talk to and listen to girls across the country—to find out what's important to them, what troubles them, what they want to know. And since 1997, I've been hearing from thousands and thousands of girls around the world who ask questions of Dr. M. (That's me when I'm the online advice columnist for the "Just 4 Girls" pages of the Girl Scout Web site: http://jfg.girlscouts.org.) And I've learned from those questions that whether you live in Dallas, Texas or Sydney, Australia, there are some growing-up questions that almost every girl has.

My two children, fifteen-year-old Robert and twelve-year-old Elizabeth, and the many friends they've had as they've grown up have allowed me to understand up close and personal what it's like to be an adolescent in today's world. Many things have changed since I was young—expectations for girls were so different then from the ones parents, teachers, and even girls hold today. Liking math (as I did) was unusual and sometimes embarrassing in the 1950s and 1960s when I was growing up, certainly not something to be proud of, the way girls today would be. Preparing for a career was not typical for teenage girls then; preparing for marriage and children was. However, so many issues are very much the same—bullies in the schoolyard, test jitters, great teachers along with really awful ones, chores no one wants to do, endless negotiations over bedtime or music and clothing choices, the desire to fit in, long conversations with best friends, anguish over betrayals, and secret crushes.

I've never forgotten what it's like to be a preteen and young teen girl. I still vividly remember my junior high school science teacher who had a violent temper (I ducked just in time when he threw a heavy tape dispenser in my direction once). I remember leaving the house in black skintight pants that my dad said should not be seen in public—at least not on me. I remember the intense crush I had on those three cute boys in the band, the ones my best friend and I nicknamed so no one would know we were talking about them (I wonder how they look and what they're doing now). And I remember how tough it was being too shy to say the right thing at the right time.

Writing this book with my daughter, Liz, has been a particularly enlightening experience, with both of us learning more about each other. You can read her introduction next.

@ @ @

Liz says: I'm twelve years old, and like my mom when she was my age, I'm shy— except when I'm dancing, something I spend a lot of time doing. My other hobbies are playing piano (although most of the time I'm not thrilled about practicing) and doing all sorts of art projects, often with friends.

I work with my mom answering some of the "Ask Dr. M" questions on the Girl Scout Web site. I write my own opinion and answer as Liz (my mom's one of the only people who calls me Elizabeth). In some ways I am very different from my mom and have totally different views on some subjects, but in some other ways we are very much alike. You'll see those similarities and differences as you go through this book. Coincidentally, my friends and I also call the guys we like weird names that somehow make sense to us. For example, one day in our Home and Careers class, a boy suddenly started singing "I'm a Little Teapot" (probably out of boredom) so his nickname became "Teapot."

Like you, I'm a preteen (or maybe you're a little older, but probably not much), so I know how you feel in certain situations, and we probably share some of the same experiences. I hope that means that every time you finish a chapter you won't be thinking something like "I'm so not doing that" or "That's ridiculous" or "What do they know?" Part of my job is making sure that my mom remembers that times have changed and that the world is not the way it was when she was my age.

I think you'll find out many things from reading this book, and perhaps most important of all, you'll learn that there's really "nothing bad about being good."

⑥ ⑥ ⑥

Now that you know a little about who we are (and you'll find out more as you read this book), go ahead and start reading. You don't have to read the chapters in any particular order—it's up to you. You might want to read straight through, or you might have a really good reason for going right to the section on bullies (has someone been bothering you on the bus or in the hall at school?) or the one on managing your time (are you feeling overwhelmed by everything that's going on in your life?). In every chapter you'll find fun quizzes (not like the ones you take in school—these don't have grades, and there are no right or wrong answers), activity ideas, and tips for learning more about yourself and your changing world. Turn the page and start taking some important steps that will help you turn your dreams into reality.

Harriet S. Mosatche, Ph.D., and Liz Lawner

Girls:
What's So Bad
About Being Good?

CHAPTER 1

Will the Real You Please Stand Up?

Coming to Terms with Your Inner and Outer Self

Do you know that you're really several people? No, that doesn't mean that you have a multiple personality disorder like some of the characters you might have seen on a TV movie or soap opera (you know, the kind of story where sweet sixteen-year-old Jane sometimes thinks she's tough Alicia and at other times manipulative Tiffany). Getting back to *you*—don't you have a wide variety of qualities, and doesn't everyone see different aspects of you? To your English teacher, perhaps you're a conscientious and serious student. To your best friend, maybe you have a wicked sense of humor. To your mom, you're a stubborn but kind kid who's not old enough to go to the mall without an adult. To your younger sister, you're the coolest person who's ever lived—except when you become a raving maniac because she messed up your room while you were out.

How Do You See Yourself?

Who are you, really? What's important to you? How well do you take care of yourself? How are you unique—different from every other person in the world (even if you have an identical twin)? That's what this chapter is about, and to give you a head start, do the exercise in the next section. Since you're going to be sharing some pretty private stuff, you may want to make a copy of the answer chart in this exercise—unless you know that this book will definitely not be available for public display (like your older brother showing it—and your answers—to his friends). Another good reason for making a copy is that you may want to complete this exercise again in a few months or even in a year or so to see how your view of yourself has changed.

Who Are You?

Give yourself just ten minutes to list a dozen answers to the question "Who are you?" Don't spend a lot of time thinking—just put your thoughts on paper as they come to you (and don't worry if you come up with fewer or more than twelve statements).

1. I am _____
2. I am _____
3. I am _____
4. I am _____
5. I am _____
6. I am _____
7. I am _____
8. I am _____
9. I am _____
10. I am _____
11. I am _____
12. I am _____

Without looking ahead in this chapter, what did you learn about yourself? Count up the number of statements that relate to:

♣ Your appearance (for example: I am short)
♣ Your friendships (for example: I am a caring friend)
♣ Your family (for example: I am Rob's younger sister)
♣ Your personal qualities (for example: I am usually honest)

What do the numbers tell you? How many of your statements were about your appearance? How many were about your friendships? Your family? Personal qualities?

Are you so focused on your looks that you've lost track of the kind of person you are? Are you so caught up in the world of your friendships that your family is not even in the picture?

Which of your answers surprised you? Do your responses provide a full picture of who you are? Anything still missing? Why do you think you didn't put those things down on paper? Are you happy with your answers? Do you like how you've drawn yourself? What would you like to change? Why? (You can find out more about setting goals for yourself on page 35.)

You can discover even more about yourself and help a good friend learn about herself if you ask her to do this activity, too. The same rules apply: twelve answers in ten minutes. (Of course, if she asks for extra time and she's midsentence, don't grab the paper from her!) Ask her to share her ideas and insights about your answers with you, and you do the same for her. Sometimes it may take someone else to help you understand yourself better. Your friend might help you realize that you left out the fact that you have a quick temper, and you might help her recognize that she's often impatient. Or maybe you hesitated to say positive things about yourself, like "I am very smart" or "I'm the best player on my softball team." Lots of girls your age are reluctant to announce how great they are, even to themselves. If you don't have lots of positives on your list, think of a couple now, and write them in the space provided on page 4. And if you do have lots of positives, it won't hurt to add a couple anyway.

I am _____

I am _____

It's obvious that you can learn as much about yourself by what's on your list as what's not.

Ask an Adult

If you feel comfortable, you can also ask an adult whose opinion you value to look over your responses. Does he or she see you the same way you see yourself? What does this person see in you or about you that passed you right by? Or maybe, that quality he or she sees is something you just put on, like makeup—something that's not a genuine part of you (that's why it wasn't on your list).

Example:

Your aunt thinks that you should have written "I am a person who always stands up for what I believe." The fact is, you don't always do it. However, because your aunt is so important to you, you want her to think the very best about you. You let her think that you do always stand up for what you believe. And you don't tell her that when a couple of friends were making fun of kids with disabilities recently, you didn't say a word—even though you knew how wrong and unfair their comments were. You weren't proud of yourself, but at that moment you believed that you would look totally uncool if you were to say something like, "It's wrong to make fun of people who are different from us." So you kept quiet, and you certainly didn't share that incident with your aunt.

Start Making Some Changes Now

A final note about this exercise: You've looked at who you think you are as well as who your friend and an adult you trust think you are. What should you do with all this information? Answer the questions below now, and you're on your way to making a couple of important changes in your life. Be sure to fill this out about qualities that can be changed. Being kind is something you have control over; being six feet tall isn't. However, how you *think* about your height is something you can change.

✿ What's *one* thing *not* on your list of I am's that you'd like to have there?

____

✿ What two things can you do to help make that happen?
1. _____________________
2. _____________________

Liz Says:

Okay, so who are you? I know you've been answering this question for the last fifteen or twenty minutes. And maybe you're tired of it. You may have loved your answers or hated them. They might have revealed a lot about you or very little. I'm not going to ask you to think about your answers again, but just think of the *question*. But this time, when you ask yourself "Who am I?" answer with a picture. Don't just put a picture to the words you've already written. Instead, in the space on page 6, draw your answer. Or, if you prefer, just keep a picture in your mind. You can draw more than one picture to represent the various ways you see yourself. And don't worry about your artistic ability. That's not what counts. These pictures will be great to look at when you are having an identity crisis, questioning everything about yourself down to the last detail. Who are you?

✿ What's *one* thing on your list you wish would disappear?

_____

✿ What two things can you do to eliminate that quality?

1. _____
2. _____

Get started—you've got some work to do!

Looking Good, Feeling Great

Your mom or your grandma or maybe some other older female relative might have told you that when she was growing up, so much emphasis was placed on how she looked that almost nothing else counted. Back then, girls were valued for their attractiveness, and often little else. Fortunately, times have changed, and girls today get the message that they can do or be anything—a pilot, a surgeon, a scuba diver, a carpenter. They can be smart and strong and assertive. But many parents may have taken things just a bit too far. They act as if their daughters will forget about becoming a doctor or lawyer or doing science projects if they are ever given a compliment about their appearance. So they tell their daughters how smart they are and how great it is to have an important career, but they ignore how their daughters look.

Here's where girls can teach their parents an important lesson about balance—the balance between internal and external beauty. It's okay to care about how you look and still care about your school grades and your relationships with your friends and family. You can both wear the latest hairstyle and be a math whiz. You can be a terrific soccer player and still care that your legs are hair-free.

Close your eyes and visualize the last time you looked really terrific. Was it yesterday? Last month? A year ago? When you were a toddler? (Come on, there have to be lots of days more recently when you liked your appearance.) Why did you think you looked good on that day? Can you capture what you were feeling? The fact is, when you think you look nice, usually you feel good. It works the other way around, too. On days when you're feeling good about yourself, you probably like the way you look. So, how you see yourself and how you feel about yourself go hand in hand. Why is that important to recognize? Because it means that when you're in a bad mood, you might be able to cheer yourself up by perking up your looks a bit. Of course, if you're in an absolutely horrible, really disgusting mood, you might be critical of your looks no matter what you're wearing or how your hair comes out. And then, more drastic action is needed.

Taking Action

Before we get too sidetracked, think about what happens when you wake up on the wrong side of the bed. What do you notice? That your hair is standing out in every direction, that your pants are too short, that you have a pimple on your cheek, that your eyebrows are too bushy? In other words, you hate how you look. And what do you typically do? You focus on the negative—what's wrong about how you look, not what's right. And it doesn't help when your mom tells you that you look just fine. In fact, hearing her say that just annoys you even more.

Do This: Here's a strategy for you to try the next time you feel that way: Take everything off—yes, everything—your clothes and any hair clips or other stuff you've got on. Put your pajamas or nightshirt back on and get back into bed. Close your eyes, and think about some of your favorite things waiting for you in your closet or dresser. For a moment or two, say to yourself, "I know how to make this day go better for me." You may be skeptical about this part, but saying it will help. Now get up, go back into the bathroom, and brush your teeth (it doesn't matter if you've already done that part of your morning routine—do it again). It's a new day. Find one of those outfits you visualized, take it out, and put it on. And fix your hair a different way—maybe part your hair on the left instead of the right or find a matching headband. And don't keep looking in the mirror.

6 6 6

The point in all this (and it's not just in terms of your appearance) is that taking action is almost always better than waiting for something to happen. This is a technique that works for your friendships, your family life, and your schoolwork. For example, if you're not doing well in school, waiting for your grades to improve won't make you do better, but changing the way you study might.

Some Things to Think About as Your Body Changes

Your appearance is probably on your mind quite a lot these days as you experience the changes that are part of puberty. Every girl goes through puberty—beginning anywhere from about eight to thirteen and not ending until you're in high school, when you will have reached your adult height. Many of the changes associated with puberty are inside your body; chemicals called *hormones* are causing your body to change in different ways.

Liz Says:

When I'm having a bad day, I always criticize everything about my looks and complain endlessly. I change a million times, try tons of hairstyles, and change anything else that I can. When you're having one of those awful days, change into an okay outfit, one that you like how you look in but isn't too fancy. If you wear something really special, you'll probably think you look bad in it, just because of your mood, and then you'll never want to wear it again. Also, don't wear something new because even if it would look good on another day, you won't give it another try.

How do you know that you've started puberty? You'll begin to grow at a faster rate, but not every part of your body will grow in the same way at the same time. So you'll probably feel a little awkward as you get used to those changing body parts. And, hard as it is, try not to compare yourself to every other girl at school. You're growing at just the right pace for you. But if you have some serious concerns about how you're growing, it wouldn't hurt to talk to your parents, your doctor, or your school nurse.

The two changes you're probably most self-conscious about are getting your period (also called *menstruation*) and your developing breasts. There are some questions and answers on pages 12–13 about these topics that may help you feel more comfortable.

Tips for Healthy, Attractive Hair

One sign of growing up is that your hair gets oilier, and you'll need to wash it more often. It's okay to shampoo every day, if necessary. To keep your hair and scalp healthy, don't share hairstyling tools like brushes and combs, or head stuff like hats and hair bands (you might not want to think about head lice, but using someone else's things is one way to spread infection). Letting your hair dry naturally is really easiest on your hair, but if you do use a blow-dryer, use a cool or warm, rather than hot, setting to prevent damage.

What about hairstyles now that you're getting older? Look through magazines—and not just ones for girls your age—to find pictures of styles you'd like to try. Show the picture to the person who cuts your hair, and ask whether a style like that would work for your hair type and your lifestyle. If you have very thick, curly hair, and the style you've selected is shown on someone with fine, straight hair, you may have to come up with an alternative plan. Or if the style you selected demands an hour of setting and styling and you usually run out of the house to catch the school bus with your hair still wet from your morning shower, you may want to keep that style for a special occasion and find something that fits your everyday life a little better.

Hair Here, Hair There

Having more and thicker body hair is one of the ways you're changing during puberty. Most girls start to shave their underarm hair and legs during the preteen or teen years, but some don't. Whether and when you start to shave and how often you do it are very individual decisions. If you're not comfortable with the idea of shaving but want hair-free legs and underarms, find out about products called *depilatories,* chemicals that you spread on the hairy area and remove in a short time, along with the hair. If you use one of these products, follow the directions carefully, and get a parent's permission before you try one of them.

Your Skin Needs Attention, Too

Oily skin and pimples are another sign of growing up. What can you do about them? Here are some suggestions:

* Wash your face frequently, with mild soap or other cleanser made especially for the face.
* No matter how tired you are, clean your face thoroughly (whether or not you're wearing makeup) before you go to bed. If you don't, you will not only make a mess of your pillow, you'll also clog your pores and allow dirt to settle in for the long haul.
* Don't pick at pimples—that's a great way to cause an infection, and it doesn't get rid of the pimples anyway.
* Use skin care products that you can get at the drugstore for mild cases of acne.
* See a dermatologist (a doctor who specializes in treating skin conditions) if you have severe acne. She or he can prescribe the stronger creams or lotions you might need.
* Remember that almost every girl your age breaks out—it's all a part of normal growing up.

Q. *When should I start wearing a bra?*

A. The right time to start wearing a bra is when you want to. And you might want to for a number of reasons: all your friends are wearing one, or you feel more comfortable being a bit more covered up, or you like the kind of support a bra gives. Your mom, older sister, or aunt might tell you that you don't need one yet, but wearing a bra is more about what you want than what you need. And with the selection of bras that you can find in stores today, you will definitely be able to find one that fits you just right—regardless of the size and shape of your breasts. That's another thing to remember: breasts come in every size, shape, and color, and they're not necessarily perfectly symmetrical.

Q. *When will I get my period?*

A. Your first period will start about a year and a half after your breasts have started to develop and your pubic hair has already begun to show. So be prepared by keeping a couple of sanitary pads in your locker at school and a box of them at home.

Q. *When I get my period for the first time, will the blood start gushing out?*

A. No, usually you'll notice a small brownish–red or pinkish stain in your underpants. That will give you time to get the pad you've already stored away, ready for this important occasion. Once you're used to getting your period, you may notice some signs that let you know that your period will begin soon—perhaps a little bit of cramping or bloating.

Q. *How often will I get my period, and how long does each one last?*

A. At first, your period may come at irregular intervals. It takes a while for your body to settle into a routine. Some girls get their periods like clockwork, exactly every twenty-eight days. For other girls, thirty-five to forty days may elapse between periods. Each menstrual period lasts from just a couple of days to a week. All of these differences are normal.

See table 1-1 for a chart you might want to copy and use to record your menstrual cycles. Or you can just use a regular calendar to note when you get your period, how long each one lasts, and any special comments that you want to remember (for instance, whether your flow was particularly heavy or cramps were severe) so you can let your parents or doctor know.

Table 1-1. My Period Chart

Start Date	End Date	Comments

Do This: Use sunscreen with an SPF rating of at least 15 whenever you're out in the sun, particularly during the time when the sun's rays are strongest—from 10 A.M. to 3 P.M. And don't expect the product to continue to work all day if you've only applied it once. Reapply often, particularly after swimming or doing activities that lead to sweating. Getting a tan is not a sign of good health—it's a sign of damaged skin. Wear a hat, cover up, and don't forget your sunscreen. Whenever you can, find a shady spot for outdoor activities when the sun is at its brightest. And if you're fair-skinned, you need to be even more careful.

Eat Well, Feel Well

You've probably been told since you were a preschooler that you should eat meals and snacks that will supply you with all the essential nutrients, such as protein, vitamins, minerals, and carbohydrates. But now that you're on the cusp of the teen years, you may think you're too old to have to follow those old rules. Wrong! Good nutrition is even more important now—you're going through a time of rapid growth, and your body needs that good stuff. Make sure you get enough protein and minerals, such as iron, zinc, and calcium, so that you can stay strong and healthy and have lots of energy. Look for books or online information that tell you which foods contain high amounts of each of the nutrients, and check out your eating habits for a couple of days to see how well you're doing. Use table 1-2 and ask a parent or teacher to help you figure out what you're getting enough of and what you're missing. But you don't need a chart or any adult's help to know that a breakfast of ten chocolate cookies with cream filling and a lunch of chips, a hot dog, and a soft drink will not move you along the path to good nutrition.

Do You Like Your Body?

Everyone's body is different. And there's no reason at all for you to try to make your body look like someone else's. As long as you're healthy and fit,

Table 1-2. My Food Diary

Day/Date							
Breakfast							
Lunch							
Dinner							
Snack(s)							

and your doctor thinks your weight is in the proper range for your body type, you're doing fine. In fact, gaining weight, filling out, and developing some curves are the kind of changes that go along with puberty. But some girls begin to diet when they're as young as nine or ten—not because their health requires it, but because they are constantly bombarded with pictures in magazines, on TV, and in the movies of actresses and models who are superthin. Some girls aspire to look just like their favorite stars. Other girls may decide to lose weight after they overhear the comments of boys at school who have no right to comment at all about girls' bodies. Some parents think they're being helpful when they pressure their daughters to lose weight. These moms and dads believe their daughters will avoid weight problems later in life if they start to diet now. But if their daughters are within a normal weight range, they don't need to lose a single pound. Other girls are told by their friends that they'd look better a few pounds lighter, and so a cycle of dieting begins to satisfy someone else's ideal.

What can you do with all these messages? Become aware that they're affecting you. But don't start losing weight just because someone else thinks you should. (Of course, if you really are significantly overweight, work with your doctor to get into a healthier pound range.) Once you develop an obsession with becoming thin enough, it's very tough to overcome it. You might develop an eating disorder—a real illness just like a cold or cancer. Girls who become anorexic purposely starve themselves, striving for a weight that is unrealistically, often dangerously, low. Bulimia is another serious eating disorder, in which people binge on food—take in large quantities at one time (like giant-sized bags of potato chips followed by gallons of ice cream and a liter of soda pop) and then force themselves to throw up, use laxatives, or exercise excessively so they won't gain weight. If you have symptoms of one of these disorders, you need professional help. And the sooner you get it, the better. If you suspect that one of your friends has anorexia or bulimia, ask your parent or another trusted adult for help. This is not the kind of situation you can or should handle on your own.

What if your problem is overeating—to the point of becoming seriously overweight? Obesity (being dangerously overweight) is a growing problem among girls as well as boys today. And if you're heavy as a preteen or teen, you're more likely to have trouble keeping your weight at a normal level as an adult. Starting a healthy diet regimen, under a doctor's supervision, is a reasonable course of action. An added benefit of getting your weight under control is that you'll probably feel more comfortable in social situations if you feel good about the way you look.

What About Exercise?

Regular exercise is not just for athletes or people trying to lose weight. It should be a regular part of every girl's routine. You may have gym in school, but how much exercise do you actually get in those classes? How often do you go? Once or twice a week? When you're in your gym class, how much time do you spend doing something active enough to get your heart rate up to a level that is considered aerobic? How much time do you spend waiting around for a chance to throw a ball or run around a track? Doctors say that you need at least twenty minutes of continuous aerobic activity three or more times a week to see some benefits. If you're not getting that kind of work-out in school, figure out how you can shift more fitness activities into your weekly schedule. What kind of exercise should you do? Any kind that increases your breathing and heart rate and that you're likely to want to do. If you pick something that bores you, it's going to be very hard for you to remember to do it when:

* You have a lot of homework
* A friend suggests a nonexercise alternative
* It's almost mealtime
* You're tired
* The phone rings
* You receive an instant message online
* Your dog is barking
* It's sunny outside
* A storm is approaching

In other words, anything and everything will be used as an excuse to avoid following through on your exercise routine. So pick fitness activities that are fun to do, and you'll do them. Look at these examples:

* Dance to the latest songs (choreograph a routine with a friend)
* Find a fitness tape with great music and interesting and varied moves
* Jump rope with a friend. Make up silly phrases and poems to help keep your jumping rhythm
* Go bicycle riding

* Ice skate, roller skate, or inline skate
* Play one-on-one basketball
* Set up an obstacle course contest and do it with friends

Add your own ideas to the list, and change your choice of activities from time to time so boredom won't prevent you from becoming and staying fit.

Remember What's Really Important

People—both kids and adults—often get so caught up in their everyday routines and minor problems that they lose track of the really important things in life. What are those important things? It depends on who you are and what you care about. Take the quiz on page 20 to help you understand your values.

Liz Says:

If you remember my introduction, you know that I love to dance. I take two hours of dance classes a week and continually dance at home, sometimes even when there's no music on—I hear it in my head. That's my exercise for the week. Well, not all of it, but most of it, anyway. Often I don't plan the dancing—it just happens (except for my classes). That's what a good exercise should be like—something you like and maybe even would do all the time even if it didn't get your heart pumping. Your exercise doesn't have to be dancing. It could be bike riding if you like doing that and tend to do it in your free time. But you shouldn't make bike riding your exercise just because you have a bike. Dancing's my thing. What's yours?

Be as honest as possible. You don't need to show this to anyone; you don't need to impress anyone. You're doing this to find out a little more about what's important to you. And why is that a good thing to do? Because the more you understand your values, the easier it will be to make decisions that are right for you. Here are a couple of examples:

* If you think that getting a good education is your key to success in life, then you're likely to study hard so you can do well in school.
* If you value friendship, you might talk to a friend who's dealing with a tough family situation instead of spending that time watching TV.

Choose the answer that describes you and your choices most closely. Even if no one answer seems totally right, pick the statement that comes closest to how you feel. And if you agree with more than one response, select the answer that you feel most strongly about.

Don't be surprised if you have a hard time making choices for some of these questions, since you probably value a lot of things. And some of the decisions you have to make now and in the future are going to pit your most important values against each other. That can be very tough. But knowing where you stand can help you make little decisions, like what to do on Saturday night, and big decisions, like what kind of career you might pursue. And understanding what's important to you will also point the way to good decisions about how you spend your time. There's no point wasting it on something that really doesn't matter to you.

The following quiz only begins to tap into your values. Here's a list of some of the more common values people hold:

* Adventure
* Beauty
* Creativity
* Education and knowledge
* Expressing yourself through art

Quiz: What Is Important?

1. What would you most like to do on Friday night?
   a. hang out with your two best friends.
   b. do extra chores around the house or for your neighbor so you can make some extra money.
   c. get a head start on your homework.
   d. it doesn't matter as long as it's something new and exciting.
   e. visit with your favorite cousins.
   f. polish your nails and try out some new hairstyles.

2. You've just earned $15 for washing and waxing your parents' cars. What will you do with your money?
   a. put it in the bank.
   b. use it for new sports equipment.
   c. donate it to a cause you believe in.
   d. take a couple of friends out for pizza.
   e. buy your mom or dad an early birthday gift.
   f. buy the sweater you admired in the store window.

3. You're home alone after school, and you've finished your homework. What are you going to do now?
   a. listen to music or practice the instrument you play.
   b. read a book.
   c. write in your diary.
   d. call or send an instant message to a friend.
   e. prepare dinner so your parents won't have so much to do when they get home from work.
   f. go outside and practice some new moves with your inline skates, scooter, or skateboard.

4. It's your mom's birthday, and the family plans to celebrate by going out to dinner, but your friend just told you she has an extra ticket to the concert starring your favorite group. What will you do?
   a. tell your friend that it's your mom's birthday and you've already made plans for a family celebration.
   b. tell your friend you can go to the concert, you know your mom will understand.
   c. ask your mom if your family can celebrate on a different night since you really want to be part of the celebration, but you also want to go to the concert with your friend.
   d. you have to go the concert—music is your life, and this is your favorite group.
   e. skip your mom's birthday celebration to attend the concert, you can't turn down an invitation to adventure.

5. A family member tells you there's mail for you. What do you hope it is?
   a. an invitation to the opening of the newest amusement park.
   b. a free sample of hair gel.
   c. a letter from your friend who moved out of the country last year.
   d. a notice telling you that you've won the school essay contest.
   e. a gift of money from your aunt and uncle who just remembered your birthday.
   f. the most recent issue of a teen fashion magazine you subscribe to.

(continues)

(continued from page 21)

6. The TV shows you most like to watch are
   a. music videos.
   b. documentaries on environmental issues.
   c. ones with lots of action.
   d. dramas dealing with family issues.
   e. whatever your friends are watching so you can compare notes with them.
   f. programs in which the bad guy gets caught and justice wins out.

   You probably already know that there are no right or wrong answers in this quiz. The answers just point you in the direction of what you value most in life. Look back at what you circled and see whether you can find a pattern. For instance, did you mainly choose the answers that related to being with friends (1:a, 2:d, 3:d, 4:b or c, 5:c, and 6:e)? What does that mean? That friendships are very important in your life, and that when you have to make choices, friends usually win. What if you selected mainly answers that related to excitement (1:d, 2:b, 3:f, 4:e, 5:a, and 6:c)? You guessed it: you love adventure—trying new things, taking chances.

❀ Family

❀ Fashion

❀ Friendship

❀ Fun

Twelve-year-old Jenny describes how she made a decision when she found two of her values in conflict: "Last year, all the students in my grade were scheduled to visit Washington, D.C., and we were asked to choose roommates. Two groups wanted me to join them. One was a group of three kids, and I would be the fourth, and the other group had only two kids. Although I preferred going with the first group, my mom encouraged me to select the second group. She explained that by joining that group, I would lower their costs for the trip because the room rate could be divided by three, instead of just two. The other group already had the benefit of having three people in it. The trip turned out to be lots of fun, and I felt that I had helped a couple of my classmates out."

❀ Helping people

❀ Independence

❀ Money

❀ Physical activity

❀ Power

❀ Recognition

Add to this list, if you can, and then use it to make up some new questions and answers about values. Share the quiz you created with friends or family members. What do you and they have in common, and how are you different? Remember, one value is no better than another one—they're just different, and that makes life interesting.

What Do You Like to Do?

Here's a quick way to learn more about your values: Start by making a list of the ten activities you most like to do:

1. _____

2. _____

3. _____

4. _____

5. _____

6. _____

7. _____

Liz Says:

I took the quiz on page 20 myself. For some questions, it was hard for me to pick just one answer. I was able to eliminate some of the choices because I knew I just wouldn't do them. What helped me to answer in some cases was that I knew what a particular statement represented. Just a few days ago, I had to do an exercise in school on decisions and values. I had to read about a situation, choose what the character should do, and tell which value the decision represented. So between this book and my school activity, I'm beginning to feel like an expert on values and decisions. But who knows what will happen when I'm faced with making my next real decision.

8. _____

9. _____

10. _____

Next to each activity, use the values list on pages 19 and 23 to describe the activity. For example, if you love to play tennis, write "physical activity" next to it. If you are very competitive when you play and dream of becoming the next Venus Williams, you might add "recognition." What if baby-sitting was on your list—how would you describe that? It depends on why you're doing it. Do you love taking care of little kids? Then you've tapped into the "helping others" value. If you baby-sit because it's the easiest way for you to make money, you know what value that represents. And if you baby-sit because you love the look of admiration you see on the faces of those little kids, one important value for you might be recognition. Of course, one activity could represent two or even more of your values.

Now that you have a better picture of what's important to you, figure out how much time you spend on those things that are very important to you and how much time you spend on those things that are less so. Over the next weekend or vacation from school, keep a diary that tracks what you do. You can fill in table 1-3 on pages 26–27 or use a separate notebook or diary. At the end of a two-day period, note how much time you spent on things that were important to you and how much you didn't. If you're not happy with the ratio of "values-rich" time (doing what's important to you) and "values-poor" time, decide on one change you can make for the next weekend, and then act on it.

The Unique You

Do you feel unique? Special? One of a kind? You are—no one else is quite like you. And that's great! You have qualities no one else has. You have an imagination shared by no one. You have dreams that are yours alone.

Complete the following sentences to express your uniqueness:

I am so proud that I can _____.

My favorite color is _____.

When I _____, I feel/felt powerful.

When I _____, I feel/felt successful.

The best lesson I ever learned was _____.

The person I consider my hero is _____.

The quality my friends like best about me is_____.

When I get older, I'm going to _____.

I love to eat _____.

The music I enjoy most is _____.

I wish I were less _____.

I wish I were more _____.

I like being _____ because _____.

I'm going to learn how to _____.

Table 1-3. Activity Chart

Time	What is the activity?	What value is demonstrated by this activity?	Mark VR (value rich) or VP (value poor)
8:00 A.M.			
9:00 A.M.			
10:00 A.M.			
11:00 A.M.			
12:00 P.M.			
1:00 P.M.			
2:00 P.M.			
3:00 P.M.			
4:00 P.M.			
5:00 P.M.			
6:00 P.M.			
7:00 P.M.			
8:00 P.M.			
9:00 P.M.			
10:00 P.M.			
11:00 P.M.			

Time	What is the activity?	What value is demonstrated by this activity?	Mark VR (value rich) or VP (value poor)
8:00 A.M.			
9:00 A.M.			
10:00 A.M.			
11:00 A.M.			
12:00 P.M.			
1:00 P.M.			
2:00 P.M.			
3:00 P.M.			
4:00 P.M.			
5:00 P.M.			
6:00 P.M.			
7:00 P.M.			
8:00 P.M.			
9:00 P.M.			
10:00 P.M.			
11:00 P.M.			

My best talent is _____.
When I'm tense I like to _____.
_____ almost always makes me laugh.

If you were honest when you completed these sentences, you can see that your way of looking at yourself and the world—your likes and dislikes, talents and interests, hopes and dreams—are uniquely yours. Your sentences are different from the way your mom or your best friend or your younger or older brother or sister or anyone else would have filled them out. You'll find that as you get older and have new experiences, you'll complete those sentences in different ways. But you'll always be one of a kind.

> Anna, eleven, describes what makes her unique: "I like sports, and I don't mind getting my new sneakers muddy. Some of my friends get hysterical when that happens to them. In fact, I like getting my hands dirty when I'm making things. And I don't like makeup, except, of course, when it's Halloween."

Fun with Hobbies

One of the ways you are unique is the way you prefer to spend your free time. Do you have a collection of some kind? Do you like to make things? Do you enjoy playing sports, on a team or by yourself?

Hobbies allow you to be creative (for instance, painting and sculpting) or to stretch your mind (reading and chess are examples). Some, like bicycling and running, help you become or stay physically fit.

No matter what your hobbies, they are fun to work on when:

- ❀ You've finished your homework
- ❀ You're bored
- ❀ You're home alone
- ❀ You're trying to figure out what to do with a friend
- ❀ You need a break

Are you interested in starting a new hobby? Here are a few to look into and some ways these hobbies can help you build skills and even make a little money.

Gardening

You can grow flowering plants from seed or from small plants. If your family has a garden outside, ask for a small area to be set aside for you to set up your very own garden. Your flowers can have a theme—all yellow or all tall—or be a way to express your artistic nature, combining different types, sizes, and colors. And gardening is great exercise—think of all the bending and stretching you'll need to do to keep your space looking its best! Weeding alone can give you a workout.

If you want to turn your gardening into a money-making venture, use the blooms that have fallen off or need to be plucked off (so others can take their place) and create dried flowers. You can buy flower-drying press kits or improvise with tissue paper and heavy books (ask an adult who's done this kind of thing to help). Once you have your dried flowers ready—and you can use leaves and stems as well—use them for note cards or pictures (covered with clear contact paper), which you can give as gifts or sell to friends, neighbors, and relatives.

Liz Says:

One of my hobbies is making clay miniatures. I make them with my friends and often on my own. Sometimes I even sell them to people my mom works with. When I go into her office, I can see my miniatures decorating desks and computers. It's lots of fun to make the miniatures, and it's usually pretty easy. I'm not trying to tell you to make miniatures as a hobby. You can do other things. But it's actually important that you have at least one hobby. You can do it when you have nothing to do, and it's something to share with a friend.

Making Miniatures

Lots of people collect miniatures. But it's even more fun to make them. One way to make these is to use polymer clay that you bake to harden. If you want a glazed look to your objects, brush on one that is specially made for covering clay and be sure to follow the directions (like keeping windows open as you work).

You might also try making miniatures out of bits and pieces of everyday objects, the kinds of things people ordinarily throw out or can be obtained very inexpensively, like toothpicks and pipe cleaners; tiny muffin tin liners; and pieces of yarn, wrapping paper, wood, and fabric. Books that give step-by-step instructions are available, but you might want to use your imagination along with the stuff you have around to get started. And since lots of people collect miniatures (they're great for dollhouses and displays), you already know there's a market for anything you want to sell—if you can bear to give away things you've spent so much time creating.

Designing Buildings by Computer

To get started on this hobby, you'll have to find the right kind of computer software. You can choose one that just allows you to design buildings or one that includes moving furniture, gardens, pictures, and even people around. This kind of hobby gives you a chance to be an amateur architect and designer (exploring careers is one of the side benefits of hobbies) and to try out new arrangements for your room at home without the effort of moving that heavy furniture.

Doing Crossword Puzzles

What a great way to exercise your mind and have fun! Crossword puzzles come in every degree of difficulty, and the more often you do them, the better you'll get. You can find them online, in puzzle books, and in newspapers. And, for an extra challenge, you can create your own—with help from computer software, if you'd like—and then test the word power of your friends and family.

Creating Web Sites

Following safety guidelines, design Web sites that showcase your talents while you learn new skills and even make some money. You can create Web sites for your family to share news with relatives who live far away, for your school (if one doesn't already exist) to keep students up-to-date on all the latest events, and even for local businesses. How do you get started? You can use software that allows you to design your own site without having to learn a special code (like HTML). However, if you want to design elaborate special effects, or if you're interested in having viewers interact with your site, you will need to learn a code such as Java Script. It's probably easiest to have someone who already knows that code to teach it to you. But if you are motivated and patient, you can learn from books on the subject.

Designing your site is only the first step. Since you want your site to be seen, you'll need to check out online services that will host it at no cost to you. You'll get a URL address that you can share with your friends and family so they'll be able to find your site on the World Wide Web. Once you become really serious about Web site designing however, you might want to invest in a domain name, one that only you have. But that costs money, and you'll have to renew your claim to that name regularly. Then you're in business.

Writing and Illustrating Picture Books for Younger Kids

If you love to do creative writing and enjoy drawing or painting, this may be the hobby for you. You can do your writing and drawing freehand or on a computer or combine the two. Just pick a topic that will appeal to young children—maybe animals or cars or trips or outer space—and spin your tale. It's a story, so you don't have to stick to reality, unless you want to. Once you've finished the writing part, go back and revise. It's rare to get the flavor and the exact words you want the first time around. That's why it's best to wait to illustrate until you're happy with the story. But jot down some notes or make a sketch or two so you won't forget a wonderful idea that bubbled to the surface as your written story was forming.

For finishing your project, you can bind the book together yourself or go to a printing shop that can do it for you. These handmade books make great gifts, particularly when they're created to capture the special interests of the child who's getting it. And, of course, you can show a couple of books that you've made to prospective customers who might order one or more for their children. You'll make sales and the kids will get a one-of-a-kind book that's been written and designed just for them.

As you go through your life, you will change inside and out. Your world will grow larger, new interests will take the place of old ones, and you will have experiences that may take you by surprise. If you keep in mind that how you see yourself is more important than how others see you and that you have control of who you are and where you're going, you're in store for some great adventures.

CHAPTER 2

Strong and Confident

Polishing Your People Skills and Learning to Lead

Sara and Trish say exactly the same thing in the same situation, but Sara gets listened to, while Trish doesn't. Know why? Sara comes across as confident, while Trish seems uncertain.

How do you appear to other people? It depends on who those other people are. You're probably comfortable standing up for yourself within your immediate family—the people who live with you. But do you also feel that way at school or with someone you've just met? Do you express your opinion, even when that means disagreeing with a friend? Would you like to be able to speak with confidence in front of a group? This chapter is about becoming more like Sara—strong and sure of yourself.

How Do You Rate on People Skills?

For the next couple of days, keep a record of the way you relate to others. You can do this by writing entries in your diary or journal, or simply by making some brief notes in table 2-1. Become aware of how other people respond to you, how and when you initiate conversations, how you answer questions, and how you act and feel in situations with people you don't know.

Table 2-1. How I Relate to Others

Who are you with?	How do you act?	How confident do you feel?	What could you do differently next time?

By keeping track of your actions and feelings, you'll begin to get a sense of what you need to work on. Some girls are very confident with their best friends, but they're shy in class, never raising their hands. Others have no problem answering in class, but their voices shake when they're face to face with a boy they'd like to get to know better. Still other girls are generally ill at ease with people under a variety of circumstances.

Although scientists tell us that some people are naturally quieter than others, it is a trait that can be changed with practice. You'd be surprised to know how many actresses and even talk show hosts consider themselves shy. But they worked at facing the world with greater confidence. And the more they practiced, the easier it got.

Do This: If you'd like to become more confident around people, start by setting a goal—just one small goal. You're more likely to be successful if you work at this skill in manageable steps. For example, your goal for the first week might be to make eye contact when you answer a question asked by an adult. Girls who are shy often find it hard to make eye contact. They look down or to the side. It's interesting that acting as if you're confident—even when you don't feel that way—will help build your self-assurance. So practice making eye contact, and soon it will become more natural. That doesn't mean you have to stare into someone's eyes the entire time you're talking. You can glance at his or her nose or chin or cheeks some of the time, but making eye contact will show your confidence. Use table 2-2 to track your progress on your goal. Making eye contact with adults is just one example; set a goal that's important to you.

Table 2-2. Meeting My Goals

	Goal
What I did	
When I did it	
How I felt	

What's Your Style?

Answer these questions to get an idea of your style of dealing with people in difficult situations:

1. Your friend borrows one of your favorite sweaters, and returns it with a very noticeable stain. You:

   a. never mention it, and work hard at removing the stain yourself.

   b. yell at her, telling her she's a slob and you'll never let her borrow anything again.

   c. point out the stain to her, and ask her to try to remove it.

Liz Says:

I consider myself a shy person. I'm usually quiet around other people, although I do raise my hand in class sometimes. When I'm around kids my age, I'm not really nervous the way some kids are, but I am quiet. When I'm with my good friends, I can really be myself, and sometimes that's the total opposite of how I appear to people who don't know me well. When I went to sleepaway camp last summer, it took about a week for the other kids in my cabin to get to know me, while they got to know others in just a couple of days. But after about a week, I was able to show the real me, and I developed some terrific friendships and had a lot of fun. So if you know kids who are shy, give them a chance to show who they really are, and if you're one of those shy kids yourself, work at becoming less shy so you can have fun being with other people.

2. Your friends are trying to choose a movie to see. One suggests a horror film. You hate that kind of movie. You:

a. loudly tell your friends that horror films are "so baby-ish" you can't imagine why they'd pick that movie.

b. say nothing and go along with your friends, even though you know you'll be scared out of your mind.

c. let them know that you'd prefer to see something else, but you'll go along this time so you can all be together. Suggest that the next time, you'd like to be able to choose.

3. It's time for student council elections at your middle school. You:

a. tell everyone you know that the other two people who've been nominated are stupid.

b. nominate yourself, explaining to your class why you are qualified to be a candidate.

c. hope someone will nominate you since you'd really like to be on the council.

4. Your parents allow your brother, who is a year younger than you, to stay up as late as he wants to on weekends, but you are told you must be in bed by 11 P.M. You:

   a. point out to your parents, in a calm voice, that their rules are unfair to you.

   b. don't say anything, but inside you're seething about how totally unfair your parents are.

   c. scream at your parents about how unfair they are.

5. While you're waiting in line to buy your lunch in the school cafeteria, a boy cuts in front of you. You:

   a. don't say anything, but you're really annoyed that now you have to wait even longer to get your lunch.

   b. say calmly, "Excuse me, you may not have noticed, but there's a line."

   c. yell out to him, "You jerk! Get in line like the rest of us!"

What do you notice about the choices? One represents an aggressive response to a situation. People who behave aggressively state their feelings, but they do it in a way that hurts others. Answers 1:b, 2:a, 3:a, 4:c, and 5:c are all aggressive responses. But there are more effective ways to relate to others. Answers 1:c, 2:c, 3:b, 4:a, and 5:b are assertive ways to respond. You've asserted your rights in an honest and direct way, but you haven't violated the rights of the other people in the situation.

What other way might you have answered? With passive responses (1:a, 2:b, 3:c, 4:b, and 5:a)? If you tend to behave passively, you probably hate conflict and may avoid it at almost any cost. But the cost may be your self-esteem. When you don't stand up for what you believe and what you need, you begin to think less of yourself.

If you often relate to your family, friends, and strangers in an aggressive way, think about why you're so angry and tone it down. Being aggressive is one sure way to lose friends, and it's certainly not going to be helpful in work situations when you're older, either. If you're passive too much of the time, practice becoming more assertive. You could role-play situations with a close friend or a parent or older sister or brother. Even though you might feel foolish doing a role-play, it will prepare you for the real situation down the road.

Keep in mind that acting assertively is no guarantee that you'll get what you want or what's fair. The person who cut in front of you in line may ignore you, and your parents may not change their rules, but you'll win anyway. Why? Because you'll feel a whole lot better about yourself when you stand up for your opinions and for what you know is fair. And others will respect you more, too.

Stand Up to Peer Pressure

One of the hardest times to be assertive is when you're dealing with peers—kids your own age. You're at a stage in your life when you really want to be accepted by your peers. It's often easier just to go along with the crowd than to stand out by being different. When everyone else is wearing their hair long, it takes courage to wear your hair short, even when a cropped look is more flattering on you and is easier to deal with in your busy schedule.

Becca, age twelve, has had lots of experience standing up to her peers. She says, "A lot of people at school don't like my friends. They have the reputation for being weird, and I guess they are a little different. But I would never stop being friends with them because of what others think. So when they get into a tough situation with other kids making fun of them, I just gently drag them away, saying 'Let's go to class, people.'"

Starting a Smoking Habit

What about when a group of popular kids at school starts smoking cigarettes and they look so cool and sophisticated? What do you do when you're offered one? You've wanted to be friends with that group for the longest time, and this could be such an easy way to join in. Or would it? It's so tempting to say, "I'll just have this one cigarette, and these kids will think I'm cool." But what happens next? The kids in that group are still smoking the next day and the next week, and now they expect you to smoke, too. Each time you go along, it gets tougher to say, "No, I'm not interested." And with cigarettes, unlike an outfit that you can just take off, it's hard to break the habit. Tobacco contains an addictive substance—nicotine—that your body quickly gets used to. Long after the people who pressured you to start smoking are out of your life, the addiction stays with you.

Ask a couple of adults who smoke about their tobacco habit. When did they start? Why? Do they want to quit? Have they tried? What you'll probably find out is that most adults know all about the long-term dangers of tobacco—the serious lung disease emphysema and lung cancer, as well as the increased likelihood of other kinds of cancer and heart disease. They know that smoking yellows their teeth, makes their breath smell bad, and wrinkles their skin prematurely. And you'll learn that they want to stop smoking, but it's much harder than they ever imagined, so they keep smoking. Adults don't smoke to be cool. In fact, many smokers these days say that they often feel like outcasts in social situations. They can't smoke at work; they can't smoke at their friends' houses; they can't smoke around children. But they still need to feed the addiction they just can't get rid of. Picture this: a group of employees shivering outside their office building on a freezing day while they puff on their cigarettes. They don't feel cool at all—they're just plain cold!

Have you ever noticed that smokers seem more jittery than those who don't smoke? Recent research studies have found that smoking, particularly heavy smoking, is linked to the development of serious anxiety disorders in teens and adults. And this association does not come about because people who are nervous use cigarettes to stay calm. Instead, scientists say that smoking may actually cause people to suffer from panic attacks, which are episodes of intense nervousness. While researchers aren't exactly sure what is happening, they suspect that the nicotine affects the brain or that the tobacco reduces the amount of oxygen available in the bodies of smokers. So, far before you have to worry about heart disease or lung cancer, you might want to think about the emotional harm cigarettes can cause.

Liz Says:

This may sound kind of disgusting, but I know it's good for you to hear about this experience I had a couple of years ago. I had visited a science museum where a pathologist, a doctor who studies tissue samples from dead people, was showing lungs from people who had died. One person had died from lung cancer, and we had a chance to look at this lung. It looked totally gross, and it sure gave everyone an opportunity to think about what smoking does to your body. I will never start smoking!

If you haven't started smoking, there's no good reason to start. You may have heard that some girls smoke to keep their weight under control. They believe that cigarettes are a substitute for food. There are far better alternatives, like gum or carrots (and many girls who smoke to lose weight are already in the right range, so their diets are unnecessary).

But maybe you're already a smoker. What can you do? Stop as soon as possible. The longer you keep this habit, the harder it is to stop. Talk to your doctor, the school nurse, a guidance counselor, or a parent—someone who can support your decision. Leaving smoking behind will be one of the most important decisions you can make for your health and your future.

Assertiveness Tips

Saying no to smoking is just one of the times you'll have to assert yourself. You may need to be assertive when a classmate asks if she can cheat off your test paper or if a friend asks you to lie to your parent and hers to cover up for her when she stopped off at the mall instead of going straight home the way she was supposed to. What other situations can you think of—or have you been in—in which being assertive would be helpful?

Here are some tips to help you in those difficult situations:

* Speak clearly and firmly. Use assertive language. Instead of "Well, I guess, maybe we can do that," say, "Yes, I would like to do that."
* Look directly at the person while you're talking.
* Ask a friend to remind you to be assertive when you revert to a passive or aggressive way of communicating.
* Don't expect too much too soon. If you start out as very passive, you won't become totally assertive overnight. Start speaking assertively in familiar situations before trying out your new way of communicating under less comfortable circumstances.
* Don't give up when you've suffered a setback. You may go through periods when you're just not feeling very positive and it's harder to be assertive. Or you may experience a couple of negative reactions to your attempts to act assertively.

How to Be Assertive Without Saying a Word

* Look directly at the person to whom you are speaking.
* Stand up straight to show your confidence.
* Smile only when you are genuinely pleased about something, not just to please someone.
* Raise your hand and arm straight up when you want to be called on in class.

❋ Practice some standard replies you can use when you're treated in a way that is not respectful. For instance, you might say something like "I will not continue this conversation unless you can start speaking to me with respect."

Do This:
Write some statements here that you can use as reminders of your value, a person who should be treated with respect. Some examples might be "I am an important person," "My opinions count," or "I deserve to be heard."

❻ ❻ ❻

_____

_____

_____

_____

_____

_____

_____

_____

_____

Speak with Confidence

Do you know that public speaking is one of the most common fears people have? So if you start to shake just thinking about giving a presentation in class, you're definitely not alone. But learning to speak with confidence is a skill that you'll need, regardless of what you do with your life. Almost any job you can think of requires good public speaking skills. Why should you think about this now? You're not about to get a full-time job or run for political office any time in the near future. But these skills will help you out right now—whether you're participating in class discussions, running for student government, or teaching a group of younger kids. Speeches allow you to voice your opinions and share information you've collected. When you're up there giving your presentation, you're in charge, and everyone else has to listen to you—not a bad position to be in.

How do you go about learning to speak with confidence? Practice, practice, and more practice. Where do you begin? Follow these steps:

1. Rate yourself right now and every couple of weeks on the following scale to monitor your progress:

absolutely   totally
terrified <---------> comfortable

2. Decide on one small action you can take during the coming week. You might start by raising your hand in class in a firm no-nonsense way straight above your head when you want to speak. Get rid of the timid, half-hidden raised arm and hand. Show your confidence before you even begin to speak. Once you've accomplished that first action, decide on a second one (perhaps giving more than one-word answers to class questions).

Liz Says:

One day at lunch my friends were playing a card game, and a boy I slightly knew started watching the game. The game got really exciting, and in a pretty loud voice, I started telling one of my friends what to do—something like "Put that card down!" This boy then said, "Liz talks—she said something. I can't believe it!" I was glad he was there to witness this event. It was a little embarrassing but funny at the same time.

3. Practice breathing exercises, which will allow you to speak with authority. Take a deep breath, filling your abdomen with air, and then exhale. Use your breathing to sound stronger.

4. Seek out an opportunity to give a brief presentation in a setting where you feel most comfortable, perhaps in your Girl Scout troop or another activity you're involved in.

5. Ask someone to videotape a presentation (not when you're giving it for real, but when you're practicing). By watching how you look and how you sound, you can learn an enormous amount about what works and what doesn't. If you will allow someone else to watch your videotape with you, that person can also make some suggestions that will help you give better speeches.

6. Volunteer to give a presentation in class. Yes, volunteer! If you don't do it, you won't get over your fear. Even if your knees are wobbling and your heart is pounding, you'll get through it, and the next time will be easier. And you will have to make sure there is a next time, and a next time after that. Before you give your speech, make sure you're prepared. The more prepared you are, the more comfortable you'll be. But don't memorize an entire speech—you don't want to sound like you're reading a report (nor does your audience want to hear one). And practice your presentation with a small, friendly group—perhaps your family or close friends—who can offer gentle, constructive criticism.

7. Keep looking for opportunities to speak up. You might find that you have unearthed a hidden talent. But don't expect to become jitter-free. In fact, a slight case of nerves is actually a good thing—you'll stay on your toes and make sure you're prepared and alert.

Becoming a Stronger Speaker

Once you are pretty comfortable with the speaking part of giving presentations, you can focus on other techniques that will add to your strength as a speaker. For example, insert humor to keep your presentation lively. That doesn't mean you need to collect a battery of jokes. A funny personal example that you feel comfortable sharing probably works better, anyway. And pay attention to your audience. When they start looking like they're a million miles away, bring them back by changing the tone of your voice, walking around instead of standing stiffly in one place, or moving on to a more interesting example or issue.

It takes years of practice to become an excellent speaker. Start now to work on your skills so you'll be ready when you really need them.

Liz Says:

I've always been nervous about doing oral reports in front of the class. A couple of years ago, when I gave reports, my knees would start to shake, and I'd feel as if I were swaying from side to side. Sometimes, I even felt that I was going to fall down. And if I had to read a report, I'd just hold the paper in front of me, reading quickly without hand motions. I knew I was boring the class, but I couldn't do anything about it. But it's gotten a little easier since I've had to do a lot of reports over the last couple of years. Experience really does help. And my reports are definitely better than they used to be. I'm still nervous when I give a report, but it doesn't show as much and doesn't affect the quality of my report. I know that I can get even better, so I'm definitely going to try some of the tips in this book. My mom often tells me that she hated giving speeches when she was my age and throughout high school. Now she loves public speaking, and she does it all the time. She's even been interviewed on lots of radio and television shows, and she actually likes doing them. I hope I can get to that point, and I'm willing to work at it.

Lead On

Do you think of a leader as someone who's the president of a club? The captain of a sports team? The head of a department? The boss in an office? The president of a school class or student government? Yes, they're all leaders, and perhaps you've held one of those types of leadership positions. But do you know you don't have to be in those kinds of positions to be considered a leader? Do people turn to you for advice? Do people listen to you when you offer your opinion? Do you have a skill that you've shared with others—anything from the butterfly stroke to jewelry making? Have you been able to help others get along better? These are just a few other ways you can be a leader.

For some girls, leadership seems to come naturally—it's second nature to them. For others, leadership is something that requires work, sometimes a lot of work. Regardless of how strong your skills are right now, you can learn to develop them further. And, you may be surprised to learn that you've already had a fair amount of leadership experiences.

What makes someone a leader? What do leaders do? They look for new ways to solve problems. Leaders don't wait for opportunities—they make things happen.

Example: Chiamaka makes things happen! Her creative juices flow when faced with a problem. Instead of resorting to the same old ideas, she experiments with different ways of conquering an obstacle. She knows that sometimes she'll make mistakes, and others might not like her ideas, but she's almost always willing to take risks.

ⓖ ⓖ ⓖ

Are you like that? Do you know someone who is?

In what other ways can you be a leader? Perhaps by imagining what could happen if . . . the principal did change the cafeteria rules, your Girl Scout troop was able to raise money for their dream trip, you and your friends could start a "Save the Environment" club at school. Leaders imagine and explore all kinds of possibilities, and they inspire others to come along for the ride— as active passengers. In fact, making others feel that they're part of a team is a key part of leadership.

Example: Jessie is not the captain of her soccer team, but she's the one who's always keeping enthusiasm high when too many goals for the other side threaten to destroy team spirit.

૭ ૭ ૭

As a team player, a good leader recognizes that sometimes someone else has a better idea than she does. And what does she do? She listens to those other ideas, promotes them, and helps the rest of the group accept great ideas wherever they come from. If an alien from another solar system joined her group and came up with the perfect solution to a problem the members were struggling with, a good leader would welcome that input and use it.

Example: Keiko is that kind of leader. She doesn't have to know all the answers. She doesn't even have to have all the questions. She is open to new solutions and doesn't act as if the only good idea is an idea that she originated. She's the type of leader who can say, "Hey, that's a great idea. Let's do it!"

૭ ૭ ૭

Leaders are role models. They're the people others look up to.

Example: Lauren knows that she may have to take the first step if change is going to happen. And she's not afraid to take those risks. She's the one who makes an appointment with the school principal to explore the possibility of changing the school dress code or the trip policy or the test schedule.

⑥ ⑥ ⑥

Recognizing the efforts and contributions of others is another piece of the leadership puzzle. Leaders understand that they can only lead if others are on the team with them.

Example: Rebecca is like that. She never hesitates to give credit where credit is due. Although she played the lead part in the school play and received a standing ovation, she made sure to compliment publicly the musicians, the members of the chorus, and the behind-the-scene people for their work in putting on the very best perform-ance the school has ever had. And she does it in the most genuine way so that everyone walks away feeling appreciated.

⑥ ⑥ ⑥

Some girls show that they're leaders only when faced with a real crisis. Instead of waiting for someone else to jump in and do something, this kind of leader takes charge.

Example: Mikaela showed that she had what it takes when she and her group got lost on a school trip. While her classmates panicked, Mikaela calmed everyone and said, "Okay, how are we most likely to find our class, or how are they most likely to find us?" Her leadership allowed the group to find the right solution. She had never before shown that kind of quality, but evidently there was something inside her waiting for the right time and place to show itself.

6 6 6

Learning to Be a Leader

Try this activity to help you realize your leadership potential. In table 2-3, write down the names of three females you consider to be leaders—they do not have to be famous. Then, describe what each one does to demonstrate her leadership and the qualities each possesses that make her a leader.

Liz Says:

In my Girl Scout troop, I'm sometimes a leader. When we're asked for ideas, I share mine, and when I have a good idea, the other girls listen to it. That always feels good. We're encouraged to come up with our own ideas, and not just go along with what the adults have already decided. We've also learned that you have to listen to others. Because we have a small group and it's all girls, everyone has a chance to have her voice heard. And you don't have to wait around forever to share your ideas. Also, I know all fourteen girls in my troop and they won't make fun of anyone.

Sometimes I help people compromise in our troop. One time we were deciding what to do for a community service project. There were a lot of good suggestions, but the girls didn't have too much information to back them up, and we were wasting a lot of time. I suggested that each person who came up with an idea research her idea. Then at the next meeting, we could vote on each of them. The girls agreed, and we were then able to move on to the next part of our meeting

Table 2-3. My Personal Leaders

Name of Leader	How She Acts as a Leader	Qualities of Leadership

Look at the actions and qualities you wrote down, and choose one—just one—to work on for the next couple of weeks.

⭐ **Example:** Perhaps you wrote that your teacher, Ms. Brody, often takes the students' perspective, rather than siding with the other teachers, when a disagreement arises. One of the leadership qualities you admire is that Ms. Brody is not afraid to go against her peers when she believes that they are wrong. How does that help you in your own leadership development? You can use her as a role model for developing the strength to act independently when a situation occurs where your values are being put to the test.

With your goal in mind, think of what you can do over the next two weeks to get there. And take at least one or two actions that will show your growing leadership skills. Describe your progress in table 2-4 or in a journal. You may find that it's not easy becoming the kind of leader you'd like to be and that you can't become a leader overnight, but remind yourself that the hard work will be worth it—leadership is a lifelong skill.

ⓖ ⓖ ⓖ

Table 2-4. Leadership Goals

Goal	Action	Date

Self-confidence does not just suddenly show up on your doorstep one day. Women who always seem so strong and sure of themselves were not born that way. Ask them, and they'll probably share some surprising information about their preteen and teen years with you. Gain inspiration from those life stories.

Recognize that your needs are as important as anyone else's, that your voice deserves to be heard, and that your ideas are interesting to others. You are a leader growing stronger and more confident.

What Is a Leader?

A leader is:

- open to new ideas
- responsible
- patient
- a team player
- interesting
- intelligent
- friendly
- creative
- flexible
- tolerant

CHAPTER 3

People to People

Nurturing Relationships with Family and Friends

The number of people in your life just keeps growing. Practically every day you meet new people. Some become friends, and some don't. Have you kept some of your friends from early childhood? Are you still friends with kids who have moved away? Do you feel close to a friend you haven't known for very long? What about boys? Are you more curious about them now than you used to be? Then there's your family—and every family is different. You may be an only child or one of ten. You might have stepbrothers or stepsisters, or you might share a mom or dad with half-siblings. Do you live with grandparents or other relatives? Maybe you spend some of your time with one parent in one home and the rest of your time with another parent somewhere else. Do you have lots of cousins or just a couple? Do some members of your family live in another state or even in another country?

Relationships can get pretty complicated. That's what this chapter is all about—relating to the important people in your life, the ones you do stuff with, share your ideas with, confide in, fight with, have fun with, and care about.

Who's Important to You?

Since you have so many people in your life, you have to make choices about who you're going to spend time with. How do you make those decisions? Usually, they just happen. Your best friend calls on Friday afternoon and asks if you want to come over. You don't have other plans, you're definitely not going to begin your homework when the weekend is just starting, and you know that you two always have a million things to share. So you quickly say yes, and you're on your way. But sometimes you do have to choose between people, and those choices can be hard to make. Then you'll have to figure out *what's* important to you along with *who's* important to you.

Example: You and your cousin have planned to go to the library together on Wednesday afternoon since you both need to find books for school reports. But that day in school, a girl you've just gotten to know—the one who's really popular—asks you to come over to her house. You know you should just say that you can't make it since you already have plans to go to the library with your cousin. But then you might miss out on what could be your only opportunity to cement a budding friendship. She'll ask someone else, they'll become close, and you'll go back to your regular boring life.

6 6 6

Life is full of choices like that—between being true to your values or taking advantage of an opportunity that might not come along again. You may want to think there's only one right answer, but usually it's more complicated than that. Working out how to deal with relationships is something that will keep you busy throughout your life.

What can you do now to help you make good decisions about relationships? Start by looking at the big picture—all the people in your life. Some will stay in it, whether you're happy about it or not. Maybe there's a really annoying relative, someone who's constantly questioning you about every single thing you do or someone who always has something negative to say, no matter what the subject is. While you might be able to keep contact with relatives like that to a minimum, it's probably not possible to avoid them totally—at least not until you're an adult.

But can you think of people who are not adding anything to your life, who are just there, taking up relationship space that could be saved for someone who would be a plus? Perhaps you've stayed friends with a girl who's always asking for favors, who only has time for you when no one else is around. Why would you continue to make time for someone like that? Because she's become a habit—someone's who's been there since you were five, and you haven't spent time thinking about weeding out people who don't enrich your life. Well, now is the time to do it. Not in a mean way, of course. Saying, "Hey, Nancy, you're such a loser. Get out of my life." is needlessly hurtful. But the longer you wait, the tougher it gets to break that habit. Find a gentle but firm way to spend less time with people you no longer want relationships with, and begin to be more open to new people. Spend a few minutes—right now—thinking about or even making a list of people who you want more time with and those you want less time with, and write the information in table 3-1. Also decide what actions you're going to take to point your relationships in a more positive direction.

Family Ties

What kinds of families do you see on television? You might watch a show in which a family problem is neatly solved each week with everyone going along eagerly with the solution within the half-hour time slot. The family members all seem to really like each other, and their behavior is so normal. Of course,

Table 3-1. Rating My Relationships

Nonworking Relationships	Actions I Can Take

they're all acting. In other shows, the characters deal with one crisis after another—enough drama to keep tears flowing for a full hour. Then there are the programs in which every family member tells jokes—or is a joke—during an entire episode.

If you haven't paid careful attention to how families are represented on TV, take a closer look. For a few days or a week, as you watch your usual programs, fill in table 3-2.

How real are these characters? Not very. But if directors and writers were to show what happens to real families, viewers would not be likely to stay tuned for very long—family life would be too boring, too noisy, too confusing, or maybe all three. So if you've been judging your family life against a television yardstick, stop! Pay attention to what's going on in your own family and figure out what you can do to keep your family ties strong. Why? Because no matter how angry you get with the rules in your house or how annoyed you get at the lack of privacy you're allowed, the bottom line is that the people in your family love you. And if you're in the kind of family situation in which there isn't a lot of love, maybe you know some other people who

Table 3-2. TV Families

Name of TV Show	Who's in the Family?	What Are the Characters Like?	Do I Know a Family Like This?

act like they're family to you. You might have a Big Sister, a Girl Scout leader, a religious adviser, or a teacher (yes, there are teachers like that) who can support you and help you grow up feeling good about yourself.

On the next few pages, you'll find some ways to strengthen family connections. See which ones might work for you and the members of your family.

Choose Your Battles Wisely

This is the kind of typical advice experts give to parents when they're dealing with their adolescent kids, but it works just as well when the tables are turned. In other words, there's no point fighting with your parents over *everything*. You don't think you need to bring your jacket to school one fall morning; they do. You want to stay at your friend's house until midnight; your parents want you home at 10:00. You prefer to save your studying until after dinner; they want you to start your schoolwork right after school. You like to watch TV while you're doing your homework; your parents think only total silence allows full concentration. You aren't interested in joining any after-school clubs; they think your life should be busy every second.

If you had to argue about each and every one of these issues, your home would be a raging battleground. What do you do? Decide which issues are critically important to you, and then present your arguments—logically and calmly. You may win on some, lose on others, and compromise on still others, but if you went ahead, preparing to do full battle on everything, you (and everyone in your household) would just be miserable all the time. Would you consider that winning?

No Family Is Totally "Normal" or Average or Typical

What you see as odd behavior in a brother or sister, someone else might view as interesting. When you think your parents are interfering in your life, an outsider might think they are showing their concern. When you see your grandparent acting in bizarre ways, your friend doesn't even notice. When your family members embarrass themselves, your friend thinks they are absolutely hilarious. When you examine your own family very closely, you often focus on the problems, but no one is looking as closely as you are. And even when they

Create a "My Family" poem. Here's an example:

My family is not like
Your family.
Friends are easier to deal with,
Arguments occur on a daily
    basis.
Maybe they don't always
    understand, but they're
Involved in my life, and share
    their
Love
Year after year

do look, they probably don't really care—they're too busy checking out their own parents and siblings.

What if a member of your family does have a serious disability or illness? You may be surprised to know how typical that is. Lots of kids have siblings who are mentally retarded—they find it harder to learn or solve problems than others their age. Some kids have a dad with a drinking problem that makes him mean and scary sometimes. Others have a cousin with a mental illness such as schizophrenia—staying in touch with reality is a constant struggle for him. Many kids have a grandmother who is suffering from Alzheimer's so she doesn't always remember to bathe or dress properly, and she sometimes says things that are really inappropriate.

Some kids find it easy to accept and talk about family members who are different. But most kids your age don't want anyone else to know about their family problems. You're already self-conscious about your family members—even when they're on their best behavior. So if someone close to you is different, you feel

Liz Says:

Some people in my family whom I love very much have a disability or a serious illness. My uncle Ian is mentally retarded and can't talk (he uses his own form of sign language) or walk (he uses a wheelchair). My family visits him two or three times a month at the group home where he lives, and he's always very happy to see us. While I don't bring Ian up in conversations with friends, when a related topic does come up, I will discuss his situation. I've learned that I don't have to be embarrassed about Ian. He is a part of our family. Even though he has a severe disability, sometimes he amazes me with what he knows. Once, when my mom asked him what an electroencephalogram was, he pointed to his head. It was only then that I learned from my mom that the word means a recording of electrical activity of the brain.

embarrassed. To make matters worse, lots of people out there, even in today's sophisticated, informed world, make fun of people with disabilities or who appear different. If someone in your family has a severe physical or mental challenge, you risk being seen as uncool when your peers find out. In reality, the people who are uncool are those who don't accept differences, those who are unkind, those who are mean and insensitive. But it may take a while for you to really appreciate that.

If you've been hiding important family facts from your friends, try sharing a little bit more with them. Your true friends will accept you and your family, no matter what they're like. And as hard as it is to accept this, your "here today, gone tomorrow" friends who have trouble accepting your whole family are really not worth hanging onto.

Make a Big Effort to Get Along with Your Sisters and Brothers

Why should you try to have a decent relationship with your siblings? Because it will be worth it as you get older. They'll be around after your parents are gone, they share your childhood history and memories, they know you better than anyone—aside from your parents (and in some areas of your life, they may know you even better), and they do love you, even when that seems unlikely.

If you have an older sister, she's someone you can learn from. You can ask her those questions (maybe, "How can you tell if a boy likes you?") you don't want to ask your parents (you don't think they'd understand) or your friends (they're your age so you don't completely trust their answers). You can also get her cool hand-me-down clothes and maybe even her help with homework. She'd know how to do the kind of math they're doing in school these days, which is different from what your parents learned. If you have an older brother, he's someone who can share his perspective on issues you may be thinking about now (maybe, what boys really look for in a girl). He can also advise you about teachers and classes and how to stand up to a bully who's bothering you. If you have a younger sister, she can look up to you. Isn't it great to be someone's role model? When you want to have some fun, she'll be the first one ready to play. If you have a younger brother, you can teach him a very important life lesson: to respect females. This may not mean much to you now, but his girlfriends (and future wife) will be forever in your debt.

If your parents are constantly comparing you to your siblings—whether it's your report cards, your athletic skills, your looks, even your personalities—let them know that this strategy is definitely not helping any of you do, look, or be better. It just creates resentment, hurt feelings, and rivalry. And that can't be what your parents are striving for. As you and your siblings get older, age differences and rivalries will become less important. Working on those relationships now will pay big dividends in the future—siblings who are lifelong friends. They have fun together, really care about each other, and help each other out when times are tough.

If your parents are divorced and either one has remarried, you may have step- or half-siblings to deal with. At the beginning of this new family arrangement, you're sharing a bathroom, maybe a bedroom, with kids you hardly know. If you're very lucky, you would have chosen them as friends. But friends go home, and these kids are here to stay. Complicating the situation is the fact that they might resent you if you've moved into their home and now they have to share everything, including a parent, with you. Try to remember that your parent would appreciate it if you made an extra effort to get along with these kids who are now part of your family.

If you're an only child, you may already have people in your life who are just like siblings to you—perhaps a cousin or a very close friend. And if you don't already have someone around your age who you feel really close to, what can you do? Work at creating that kind of bond. The key word here is *work*. Relationships need to be nourished. They don't become strong just because you want them to. What does that work entail? Maintaining regular contact—through e-mail, phone calls, or real-life visits—is crucial, as is giving as much as you're taking (and that doesn't mean money or other things).

In table 3-3 or in your journal, describe a couple of instances in which you gave something (focus on qualities like time or affection or encouragement) to a sibling (or someone who is as close as one) and examples of times when your sibling gave something to you. How did you feel each time?

Make Time for Your Family

It's so tempting to spend every free minute with friends. They don't urge you to do your homework when you would rather send instant messages online. They don't compete with you to get your parents' attention. They don't insist that you keep your room clean and organized. However, spending time with your family does have significant benefits, and if you give your family a chance—the way you used to when you were younger—you might find

Table 3-3. Giving and Receiving from Siblings

What My Sibling Gave to Me	What I Gave to My Sibling

that they can be fun, too. But what can you do with your family? Write some ideas in table 3-4. If you need some inspiration, here are some suggestions:

* Talk to them. Tell them about what happens at school, about your hobbies, or news about friends. You probably can't find a better audience. Your parents, in particular, are really interested in hearing your opinions and ideas.

* Go to a movie together. If your siblings are much older or younger than you, it may be tough finding a film that you'd all like. Just keep in mind that this is not the only movie you'll ever get to see, and compromise. The important part is that everyone is doing something together—and you do get popcorn. If you can't agree on a movie, what about a play or a concert? Is the circus in town?

* Do chores together. This is probably not your dream way of spending your time, but if you have to do chores around the house anyway, why not try doing them together. Put on some music, grab a dust rag, take out the vacuum cleaner, and get to work. The chores will get done quickly, and you might even have shared some conversation or a joke or two.

* Make something with and for your family. You could put together a family photo album or scrapbook, create a Web site, or videotape a series of interviews. You'll have fun doing this activity, and you'll have even more fun looking at your creation years from now. Yes, you really did say that—the evidence is all on tape. And your sister will be reminded that she did think that her striped top was the perfect match for those checked pants!

* Play board games. This is the easiest thing to do—after you've gotten past the hard part of agreeing on which game to play. Your mom prefers word games, so she's partial to Scrabble, while your brother wants a game, like Trouble, that moves a little faster, and your grandfather is still intrigued by the challenge of buying hotels on his Monopoly properties.

❀ Eat out at a restaurant. What could be more relaxing for everyone than a meal prepared and served by someone else? It doesn't have to be fancy or expensive. No one has to think about clearing the table, doing the dishes, or scrubbing the pots and pans. And there's less temptation to argue since you're all out in public. You can use this time to share your latest news or to have your questions answered in a relaxed manner.

❀ Explore a new place. Maybe you'd like to see the sculpture garden at a local college that your friend's family visited, or explore the beach in winter, or take a hike when the leaves are changing colors. No matter how long you've lived in your town or city, you'll be able to come up with new places to visit. But you and your family will have to do some planning during the week to learn about what's going on and, more important, to make sure there's time for exploring on the weekend. That means working together to get the chores and homework out of the way. See what you and your family can come up with as places to visit. Then cooperate so you'll actually get there.

Table 3-4. Family Fun Chart

A Liz Quiz: How Much Do You Really Know About Your Parents?

Take this quiz to find out—with either your mom or your dad (or both) in mind.

Full name at birth _____

The year she or he was born _____

Where she or he grew up_____

Nickname _____

Number of brothers and sisters _____

Favorite relative as a child _____

Favorite relative now _____

Favorite book _____

Favorite food _____

Favorite vacation _____

Favorite holiday _____

Favorite song _____

Favorite celebrity _____

Favorite ice cream flavor _____

Neat freak or slob?_____

Now ask your parent to complete the quiz, and compare the answers to yours. If you match on eleven or more answers, you know your parent very well. Between five and ten right? You've got the basics down, but now you know how much you didn't know. Four or fewer? What do you think that means?

True Friendships

Do you have lots of friends or just a couple of close ones? Are you happy with the number and type of friendships you have? Would you like to make more friends? What qualities do you look for in a friend? What kind of friend are you? Take the quiz on page 68 to find out. Your feelings may not fit neatly into either the a or b answer each time, but complete the sentences in the way that seems to represent you best.

Working at Friendship

Now that you've identified those areas where your friendship skills are strong, take a closer look at those areas that need work. Keep in mind that friendship is a relationship between two people. If either you or your friend do most of the work, your friendship will suffer. If you're the one with the heavier load, you're going to get pretty tired. Carrying around all that resentment can be exhausting.

Do This:

Before you end a lopsided relationship, consider initiating a talking-it-all-out session. If the two of you have a lot in common, have fun together, and care about each other, neither one of you probably wants the friendship to end. Explain as honestly as you can how you feel—it will not be easy—and see how she reacts. The best that could happen? You'll have a more satisfying relationship in the future. The worst? Your so-called friend gets so angry about what you've told her—no matter how honest and sensitive you were—that she walks out of your life. While that may be painful, continuing a relationship where you do most of the giving and someone else does most of the taking doesn't do much for either your social life or your self-esteem.

⑥ ⑥ ⑥

You don't have control over what your friend does (although you can make suggestions), but you are responsible for what you do. By looking at your answers to the Friendship Quiz, you may discover some areas where you're the one who's a little (maybe even a lot) weak. Perhaps you are not as considerate as you could be. It's very easy to take advantage of people you've known for a long time. After you've been friends for several years, you expect that they'll just hang around, no matter what you do. So you arrive late and don't call when you're supposed to meet them. Or you cancel plans at the last minute. Or you use your nastiest tone of voice and say not-so-nice things when you're in a bad mood, and you don't bother apologizing. Does any of this sound like you? If so, what actions can you take to become a better friend? Use the planning chart in table 3-5 to set out a series of steps you can follow. *Then do them!*

Table 3-5. *How Can I Become a Better Friend?*

Step 1	
Step 2	
Step 3	
Step 4	
Step 5	
Step 6	
Step 7	
Step 8	
Step 9	
Step 10	

Friendship Quiz

1. When my friends need someone to confide in, they:
    a. avoid me, since I'm not very good at keeping secrets.
    b. turn to me, since they know they can trust me.

2. When my friends are planning something fun to do:
    a. they turn to me for suggestions because I often come up with good ideas.
    b. they don't wait for suggestions from me because I usually just go along with whatever the group decides.

3. When I'm with one of my friends, we spend most of our time:
    a. making fun of friends who are not there.
    b. doing something we both enjoy.

4. When a friend has made plans with someone else:
    a. I beg to be included.
    b. I understand that friends need to make time for other people in their lives.

5. If a popular girl in school asks me to do something for a time when I already had plans with a friend:
    a. I immediately change those plans—who knows when I'll have this opportunity again?
    b. I explain that I already have plans but would love to get together another time.

6. When my friends and I set a time to get together:
    a. I'm usually ready on time. I don't like to wait—why should my friends?
    b. they almost always have to wait for me.

7. When my friends come over to my house:
    a. we take turns deciding on what we will do.
    b. I make the decisions—after all, they're at my house.

8. If one of my friends makes a mistake or is inconsiderate:
    a. I can never forgive her—time to start looking for new friends.
    b. I prefer to talk over the situation to save the friendship.

9. When my friends and I are talking:
    a. I enjoy sharing stuff about myself, but I also like to listen to what they have to say.
    b. I do most of the talking—I've got so much to tell, and I like being the center of attention.

10. When one of my friends needs help:
    a. I let her know that I already feel overwhelmed with my own problems.
    b. I do what I can to be of assistance, without making her feel guilty that she asked.

Scoring: If you're a really great friend, you would have chosen most of the following responses:

1b: You can be trusted with your friends' secrets. (Of course, if you believe that keeping a friend's secret might jeopardize her health or safety, you must tell a parent or other adult.)

2a: You are creative and know how to have fun with friends.

3b: You respect your friends—even when they're not around.

4b: You know how to share your friends with others.

5b: You are loyal to your friends.

6a: You are considerate of your friends.

7a: You know how to play fair with your friends.

8b: You don't hold your friends to impossibly high standards—you know how to forgive when necessary.

9a: You understand the give and take of friendships—you don't have to be the center of attention all the time.

10b: You are willing to help friends, even when it's not convenient or easy.

Make a Best Friends Forever Scrapbook

If you are fortunate enough to have a very special friendship, celebrate it.

Do This: Make a Best Friends Forever scrapbook and give it to that special friend on her birthday or to mark an occasion like graduation. Get started by collecting a bunch of photographs of the two of you together. Have you saved copies of notes or letters you've

Liz Says:

While I love being with my friends, it is possible to be with a friend too much. You spend so much time with her that she becomes like a sister. Sometimes this can be good, but not always. At camp this has happened to me. I've been going to the same sleepaway camp for three years, and every year there's been someone who's been kind of like that. During my first year, it was my bunkmate who I'll just call F. She was really nice and the only person in my cabin who I became really close with that summer. But she was very messy, and I had to help her clean up a lot. It got really annoying because she often made us late for our activities. I didn't actually argue with F, but I did in my mind. That means that I felt the feelings that you feel toward someone when you fight with her, but you don't tell her how you feel or actually yell and fight with her. It's all inside—maybe not such a good thing. But I guess she didn't feel enough like a sister for me to be totally honest with her.

During my second year, it was my best friend I'll call A. She is one of the greatest friends in the world, but she got on my nerves at written to each other? Pieces of those could go into the scrapbook. Do you both love a particular type of candy bar? Add the wrapper to your collection. Include quotes from poems or books that you've discussed as well as ticket stubs from movies or a sports event you enjoyed together. What about cut-outs from magazines with brand names from sneakers or clothing the two of you both like? Use your imagination to expand this list.

You can use either a store-bought scrapbook or make one of your own, perhaps with construction paper and fasteners. Once you've collected every-

---

camp. During the last week of camp, we fought (with words) or got angry with each other nearly every day. Usually it was about the same thing over and over again. There had been a rumor going around among my friends that I liked this guy that past year. I actually didn't like him, but I couldn't convince my friends to believe me. At camp, A told all the girls in my cabin about how I liked this boy, even though she knew I didn't. If she had just told the kids in my cabin once and that was all, it would have been fine. But she had her yearbook and showed them the picture, too. Every time something was mentioned that had anything to do with a boy or school or anything even remotely related, A would bring up this boy again and tease me. At camp, there weren't that many places where I could go and be alone, but I found one. Going there helped me. I just needed some separate time and a place where no one would follow me. A didn't go back to camp the next summer, but I did. And A and I are still great friends. After that summer, we kind of forgot about what happened. Or, at least we didn't let it interfere with our friendship. Sometimes you just need to forget about what happened. And I'm really glad that A decided to go back to camp with me this year.

thing, figure out how you want the stuff arranged. You could organize them either by date (going from earliest to the most recent) or by some other theme (perhaps by places you've visited). Use glue or double-stick tape to attach your photos and other items to the pages. An important part of your scrapbook will be your cover. You might decide to get an enlargement of a favorite picture of the two of you or you might prefer to combine an illustration with your names hand-lettered in fancy writing. This is sure to be a gift that your best friend will treasure forever.

Being Popular

Girls your age can easily identify the kids at school who are considered popular. Are you one of them? If not, is it important for you to be popular? Some girls will do almost anything to be popular—maybe because they think that being popular will make them feel better about themselves. But will it? Probably not. When a girl is popular, other kids believe that everyone wants to sit with her at lunch or that she gets loads of invitations to parties or that everyone really likes her. Is that so? Not necessarily. It's more a matter of perception than anything else. Kids might think she gets invited everywhere, but sometimes girls who are popular are intimidating or unapproachable. That means that sometimes a popular girl actually gets fewer invitations because kids don't think she'd bother to go to their parties—she would have better things to do with her time. Strange, isn't it, that a popular girl might actually be lonely? Of course, some popular girls do have lots of good friends. That's because they possess the kind of qualities, such as compassion, loyalty, and fairness, that are the basis of true friendship.

Now, here's the important question: Do you want to be popular or do you want to have good friends, people who truly care about you? Are you secure enough to answer that friendship means more than popularity? That's a goal worth striving for.

The Boys in Your Life

Have you started paying a little more—or maybe a lot more—attention to boys? The very same boys that you and your friends thought were obnoxious, rude, awful, and horrible in third grade have suddenly turned into cute and funny guys. And many of them have changed their opinions of you and your friends, too. You're going through a stage when trying out romantic relationships is typical. But maybe you're not interested in boys—you're more focused on your friends, your schoolwork, or hobbies. That's normal, too.

Every middle school and junior high has its own system of "going out." What are the rules for these rituals in your school? In some places, going out merely means that you and a boy are linked by name—the kids at school say, "Jessica and James are going out." Sometimes, going out is a bit more involved—Leo and Maria sit together in the cafeteria. Or it could mean that Chelsea and Brian hang out together every day after school. Often the two people

Liz Says:

I used to be best friends with a girl who is now really popular. She wasn't popular then because we were too young to be popular or not popular. Now she's really snobby, which is one of the reasons that I'm not friends with her anymore. She used to be very nice and fun, and sometimes she still is, but she can also be very mean. When I talk to my friends about how I used to be friends with this girl, they hardly believe me. "How could you ever be friends with that snob?" I know that she's definitely changed a lot since the time when we were best friends—changed in a bad way. But not all popular girls are like that. In fact, I'm friends with two girls who are kind of popular, and I wouldn't be friends with them if they weren't nice.

involved do not arrange the logistics of dating by themselves. Friends are brought in to negotiate, to find out who likes whom. Adrienne calls Tommy to find out whether he would be willing to go out with her friend Laura. Or David sends a note to Sarah inquiring on behalf of Jason. It can get very complicated!

The one thing people are most afraid of in terms of social relationships is rejection. Fitting in is crucial during the preteen and early teen years. So if having a boyfriend is part of the social scene, you probably want one, too. Think about your reasons. Do you want the kids at school to say that you and this boy are going out so that you'll be accepted—even though you may not really like him at all? Do your parents encourage you to do things to be popular, maybe because they were never popular at your age? Do you think you should get your first dating relationship over with so your friends won't nag you any longer about getting a boyfriend? How good are these reasons for going out? Not very. They have nothing to do with what you want or how you feel, what your interests are, or what you're ready for. What about if you like being with a certain boy because the two of you share a lot of interests and you feel comfortable talking with him? Does that seem like a better reason for going out? It should.

Many girls don't want to be rejected, so they wait for a boy to ask them out. More confident girls, however, do the asking themselves. (Remember those tips from chapter 2 on becoming more confident?)

Are these relationships during the preteen years likely to last more than a couple of weeks or months? Not usually. Friends are often called in to tell someone that she or he has been "dumped," while sometimes, the breaking up is done online or by telephone. At some schools a plastic bandage with the word *cut* written on it is given to the girl or boy who is being cut. To save face, the person who has been dumped or cut may say that he or she was the one who broke up the relationship, or he or she may describe the situation accurately but use it to gain sympathy from friends.

While these early dating experiences may seem innocent enough, they can be scary and uncomfortable. And if you have had repeated experiences with rejection, you may be afraid to try again for a long time.

Many girls want to know how old they should be before they get involved in boy–girl relationships. The age to start dating depends on lots of factors:

* ❋ Your readiness (how comfortable do you feel?)
* ❋ Your parents' rules about such things (every family has different standards)
* ❋ Who the boy is and what he's like (do you share values or interests?)
* ❋ Are you attracted to him? Does he have a terrific personality?
* ❋ The boy's age (Getting involved with someone your age is almost always a better idea than going out with someone older—an older guy will have expectations for the relationship that are bound to be different from yours. This is true whether you're twelve or seventeen.)

Keeping a diary or writing in a journal can help you deal with some of your confusion and your questions surrounding boy–girl relationships. And if you can talk over your concerns with your mom or an older sister or cousin, that's great. Looking at table 3-6 may help you make good decisions about going out. Add your own bad and good reasons to the list.

What Do Boys Like in Girls?

Just as every girl is an individual with different interests and preferences, boys, too, have a variety of likes and dislikes. Here's a sampling of what some boys said when asked to discuss their feelings about girls and relationships and about the kind of girls they like:

Danny, eleven: "When I was eight, I thought girls were stupid. I wasn't interested in them at all. Now I like girls, depending on who they are. Sometimes, boys are mean to girls when they like them—not real mean, just mean in a joking sort of way. I'm not like that, but some boys are. I like sports, so I like girls who like sports. The girl I like now plays baseball, basketball, and soccer. I definitely don't like girls who are spoiled."

Table 3-6. Reasons for Going Out With _____

Good Reasons	Bad Reasons
You like him	You don't want to hurt his feelings by saying no
He respects you	Your parents want you to date him
You have fun together	Your friends think he's the coolest guy at school
He doesn't take you for granted	He's already asked you out ten times, and each time you've said no
You feel special when you're with him	He likes you, even though you don't really like him in a romantic way
You're attracted to him	You want a boyfriend because all your friends have one

ⓖ ⓖ ⓖ

Josh, twelve: "I've had girlfriends since I was ten. Actually, I had my first crush on a girl when I was in the second grade. I've always liked girls as friends. I know that girls talk about boys all the time, but boys talk about girls a lot, too. I'm interested in a girl's looks, but I'm also interested in how she acts. She should be funny, not too snobbish, not too talkative, but not too shy. I also don't like girls who are too sensitive. Sometimes, I'll be joking around, and a girl will take what I say too seriously and be all upset. That's too sensitive for me."

ⓖ ⓖ ⓖ

Martin, thirteen: "I've had three girlfriends. My first, in sixth grade, lasted three months. I broke up with her because she wasn't very nice to my friends. I tried to fit in with her friends, but she didn't do the same for me. In the beginning of seventh grade, I went out with a girl for two months. When I told her that it would be better for us not to be boyfriend and girlfriend any longer, she was very upset. I tried to talk to her to make her feel better, and I asked her friends to talk to her, too. The third girlfriend I had broke up with me on the phone, but it didn't bother me too much since I was thinking of cutting her. I like girls who have a good sense of humor and who are nice. Looks are not that important. Probably the most important reason for liking a girl is that I find out that she likes me."

Liz Says:

Last weekend, at a sleepover with the fourteen girls of my Girl Scout troop, we were playing a game of Truth or Dare. We had already done a round of dare, so we decided to do a round of truth. We knew that everyone would ask the same question—Who do you like?—so we decided to just go around the room with everyone telling which boy she liked. One girl didn't answer since she was trying to get to sleep. Another said she didn't like anyone, and a third girl said we wouldn't know who the boy was. Everyone else answered truthfully. After each person said who she liked, at least one girl would say something like "I used to like him" or "He's really cute." I thought it would be hard for me to admit who I had a crush on and that I would be embarrassed later on. But instead, I actually felt closer to this group of girls, since I now knew one of their secrets and they knew one of mine. So, boys actually brought us closer together.

Jay, thirteen: "I've never had a girlfriend, but I'd like to. There's one girl in my social studies class I have a crush on, but I'd never ask her out. I have no chance with her. She's the prettiest girl in school and she's smart. I do have friends who are girls. I like to talk with them. With my friends who are boys, we're more likely to do things, like play sports. I like girls who are lively, funny, good-looking—not like a supermodel—but they shouldn't be 'ugh.'"

ⓖ ⓖ ⓖ

Rob, fifteen: "When I was eleven, I asked my friend to find out if a girl I liked would go out with me. Once I knew that she would, I asked her out. Then we didn't talk for two weeks. It was very awkward since our friends kept trying to get us to act like boyfriend and girlfriend. I couldn't bring myself to break up with her, so I asked a friend to tell her that the relationship was over."

It's Party Time!

One of the easiest ways to learn to feel comfortable with boys is to spend some time as part of a group with them. With a friend or two, host a party and invite girls and boys you know pretty well as well as kids you'd like to know better. Before you get started with your plans, be sure your family has given permission and at least one adult will be around during the time of the party to help you keep everything under control. Figure out what the party will cost, and how you will pay for it. (Are you expecting your parents to take care of everything? Do they know that?)

Get your whole plan down on paper so you can check tasks off as you complete them. If you've prepared well, you'll be able to relax and have a great time once the party begins. If you've been careless about planning, neither you nor your guests will have fun. Running out of food, drinks, or activity ideas will make your party memorable, but unfortunately not in the way you'd like it to be.

Your Social Comfort Zone

As you get older, you will find yourself in more and more social situations—everything from parties to conversations with the parents of your friends to job interviews. A few lucky girls seem to know just what to say and how to act, no matter where they go and who they're with. But most girls need practice—lots of it. If you're one of the lucky ones, enjoy your natural social skills, and think about helping others who may not be so fortunate.

If you're part of the 95 percent of girls who find it a little tough to go to a party where you don't know anyone or who don't look forward to interviewing for a baby-sitting job, here are some tips that may help you feel a little more comfortable:

❋ **At a party where you don't know anyone except the person who invited you, and she doesn't have time to take care of you:** Look around to find someone else who doesn't seem to know other people. You'll recognize her because she's sitting or standing alone, and she'll be really glad to talk to you. Also worth a try is asking your host if you can help carry out some food or serve beverages. You'll feel less awkward

Party Ideas

- Rent some videos, and have lots of popcorn on hand.
- Hold an end-of-school-year party, with prizes for the best teacher imitations.
- Have a 1950s, 1960s, or 1970s party with decorations, food, clothing, and music from the era you selected. Ask parents and grandparents to help—they'll probably love getting involved.
- Take advantage of nice weather, and have a picnic.
- Walk together to raise money for a good cause, and then celebrate completing the course.
- Volunteer to prepare a party for older people at a community center or nursing home.

when you're doing something. And someone is bound to start a conversation with you, even if it's just about the kind of soft drink you're pouring or what's in the vegetable dip or whether the popcorn is plain or buttered. You might be able to make the transition from talking about popcorn to discussing the latest movies without too much difficulty.

* **At a job interview:** Always prepare before showing up. How? Ask a friend or, better yet, a parent or another adult who can take you and the situation seriously, to ask you some practice questions. Even if the interviewer doesn't ask the exact same questions, you'll be ready with some good-sounding phrases, and you'll have practiced presenting yourself in a poised, enthusiastic way. Nobody wants to hire a tongue-tied, unhappy person as a baby-sitter.

* **When talking to the parents of your friends:** Remember that it's definitely in your best interests to make your friends' parents your allies. You might actually need them to support you when you disagree with your parents about a curfew or your choices in clothing. What can you do? Start by answering their questions with more than a nod, a grunt, or a yes or no. Then go on to expressing interest in or asking a question about an item in their house or an article of clothing they're wearing or a project they're working on. Your parents will love hearing from their friends about how friendly and mature you are. And you will have gained some valuable experience that you'll be able to use in other situations later on.

As your social world continues to grow, you'll need to make sure that your people skills keep pace. The simple behaviors that worked when you were younger are no longer enough as you navigate your way through more complicated situations. Practicing how and what to say and do in safe and comfortable environments—think "family" and "close friends"—is a great way to prepare for the challenges that you're discovering during your preteen years and that you'll face as a teenager and beyond.

CHAPTER 4

Don't Mess with Me!

Conquering Challenges with Smart Choices

As much as you may want to avoid thinking about situations that might be unpleasant, uncomfortable, even dangerous, they will occur in your life. Maybe you've already found yourself in a tough spot or two. For example, have you ever gotten an obscene phone call or e-mail message? Has someone at school or on the bus threatened you? Have you been home alone when someone came to your door demanding that you open it?

Whether or not you've already dealt with these or other difficult situations, the worst thing you could do would be to just hang around waiting for something bad to happen. Being prepared, knowing how to protect yourself—both mind and body—and making good decisions are important ways to take care of yourself. Learning how to keep yourself safe in tough situations and treating others with respect is what this chapter is all about.

How Prepared Are You for Tough Situations?

Answer each of the following questions to see how much you know about taking care of yourself. After reading the complete chapter, review your answers, and see what you would change. It would also be a good idea to discuss your responses with an adult you really trust—either a parent or someone else.

1. You're home alone and the doorbell rings. You are not expecting anyone. You look through the peephole and see a man in a delivery uniform. What do you do? Would you act differently if he weren't wearing a uniform?

2. You're walking home from school with a friend when she takes a cigarette and matches out of her backpack and lights up. She asks if you'd like to take a puff. Sensing your reluctance, she says, "Nothing can happen to you with just one puff." What do you do?

3. A boy is walking behind you in the hallway at school with some of his buddies, and he pulls at the back of your bra and lets it snap back. He and his friends laugh. What do you do? Would you act differently if he were alone or if you were with your friends?

4. You've spent the evening baby-sitting a young child. When the child's parents come home, you can smell alcohol on their breath. The father says he's ready to drive you home. What do you do?

5. Almost every day at school for more than month, a girl in your class has been teasing you about what you're wearing, how your hair looks, who your friends are, or what you said in class. You've tried to ignore her, but you're beginning to dread going to school. What do you do?

6. At a sleepover at your friend's house, you're reading in bed, when her dad comes into the room and gives you a goodnight hug. You feel very uncomfortable since his action seems like more than just a friendly gesture. What do you do?

7. You and your friends are hanging out in the playground during recess, and one of your friends starts making very loud comments about some of the boys who walk by, things like "nice butt." Everyone is laughing and having a great time. What do you do?

8. When you come home from school one very cold afternoon, you're really hungry and in the mood for some good hot soup. Your mom is not going to get home for a couple of hours, but you know how to open a can and heat up the soup, so you figure it can't hurt to go ahead. You know that your mom doesn't allow you to use the stove when no adult is around to supervise. But hot soup is awfully tempting. What do you do?

9. You have a tremendous crush on an incredibly cute boy in your class. You've heard that he's had several girlfriends already and that the way these girls get to go out with him is that they're willing to do sexual "stuff" with him. What do you do?

10. You're tired of being bullied by older, bigger kids. One day at lunch, you see your chance to get rid of a little of the resentment by bullying a small, shy girl who is sitting by herself at a nearby table. What do you do?

Have you ever been in any situations like these? Have you always felt good about how you acted? Maybe you did or said something that you now realize was mean or even put you in danger. Perhaps you knew, even at the time, that you should have said or done something differently. You got caught up in the situation, or it was just too hard or too embarrassing to stand up to an adult or a friend or a classmate or a neighbor, someone you see all the time. These are not easy situations to deal with. The fairest and safest course of action is often the most difficult to carry out. If you ever acted in a way that you're not proud of, that's the past. Focus on the future. Instead of obsessing about what you did wrong or should have done or how ashamed you feel, decide what you're going to do the next time.

Sexual Harassment

Situations 3, 6, and 7 on page 82 describe examples of sexual harassment. It's a form of bothering another person by unwelcome touching or grabbing, gestures, stares, jokes, or comments that focus on sex or certain physical characteristics.

Example: While you're making your way through the crowded hallway to get to your class, you notice a boy brushing up against you. You wonder, "Was he trying to feel my breasts or my behind, or was it just an accidental touch?" When it happens a second time, you know that you're being sexually harassed, even if the boy acts like he's totally innocent.

Here's another example: A boy might think that he's giving you a compliment when he yells out in the hallway at school, "You have the greatest legs in sixth grade." But that kind of attention is usually embarrassing, not flattering. It's not that you never want a boy to notice your legs, but what's appropriate when it comes from a boyfriend in private is inappropriate when it comes from a boy yelling about your body in a very public setting.

6 6 6

Sometimes, when you first get sexual attention from a boy, it may seem kind of cool. But when attention turns into harassment, it's far from cool, and when an adult is doing the harassing, it's even more threatening. Boys or men who harass are violating your right to feel comfortable. But they may not realize how girls feel. A boy may think he's being funny or trying to show a girl that he likes her. He may be confused because he may have seen other boys act this way to get a girl's attention, and he's just following what he has observed. But maybe he's aware that it's hurtful and he doesn't care. Boys can learn that making girls uncomfortable, whether by touch or talk, is not innocent. It's not a decent and fair way to get a girl's attention. It's *sexual harassment*.

What if you don't know whether someone is just flirting with you or whether you are really being harassed? How can you tell the difference?

Flirting feels good; harassment does not. Flirting makes you feel better about yourself; harassment makes you feel humiliated, angry, and scared. Pay attention to your thoughts and feelings—they can be a good guide to what's really going on.

What Can You Do About Harassment?

Unfortunately, sexual harassment happens to a lot of girls, maybe even most girls. That doesn't mean that most boys sexually harass girls. But boys who harass girls usually bother many girls, not just one. Do you have to put up with it because it's something boys just do and they don't mean any harm? Absolutely not! Sexual harassment is wrong. It's unfair. It shouldn't happen to you. What can you do? Here are some suggestions:

* Tell the harasser to stop, to leave you alone. Say that you don't like what he's doing. Use your firmest, most confident voice. Be *loud* if you feel comfortable doing that.
* Talk to a friend. Ask how she deals with situations like this. If you like her advice, act on it.
* Avoid situations where you might be alone with the harasser.
* Keep track of when, where, and how you've been harassed, so if you're questioned, you'll have the facts ready to work for you.
* Tell your mom or dad or another trusted adult what has been happening to you. While you might feel embarrassed, remind yourself that you are not to blame in any way for the harassment.
* Talk to a school counselor or teacher. Many of them have been trained to handle complaints about harassment. File a formal complaint, if necessary.
* If the harasser is an adult or if you have been physically threatened or hurt, act immediately by talking to a trusted adult. You don't have to deal with situations like this on your own.

What if you're not the one who's being harassed? Maybe it's your friend or a classmate. What can you do? First, you can listen when a friend asks for advice. Then, help her to see what her options are and support her when she decides to follow one particular course of action. Don't act on her behalf—that will only serve to make her feel even worse about herself. If your friend decides to go to a school administrator, you can help her write down exactly what happened and when. Ask her questions to help her remember what the harasser said, when he said it, what she felt, and what she did.

Liz Says:

When I was in the sixth grade, the girls and boys were separately shown a videotape about sexual harassment, probably because the teachers thought it would be easier to have a discussion if we were separated. What I remember most was that a lot of the kids laughed at how the narrator pronounced the word *harassment,* but one important point that the tape did make was that both boys and girls could be harassers.

Could You Be a Harasser?

What if you're the one who's been harassing someone? While many more girls than boys are harassed, some girls do go beyond mutual flirting to harassing boys they like or those people who are not likely to fight back. Look carefully at your own behavior—it's hard to admit that you've hurt someone or made someone feel uncomfortable. Now that you know better, *stop*. Most boys who are harassed are too embarrassed to do anything about it. They think they have a reputation to uphold. But you can look at how you've acted and why, and resolve to put an end immediately to behavior you know is wrong.

Dealing with Bullies

Eleven-year-old Lauren is minding her own business walking up the stairs to her classroom when Brenda, who's a year older, starts to whisper to her friend. But it's a stage whisper, clearly meant for Lauren's ears. "Did you see what Lauren is wearing today? Where did she find that outfit—the thrift shop on Main Street? Or maybe in the garbage dump?" They walk away giggling, while Lauren is left to cope with her hurt feelings. Why would Brenda say such mean things? Because she's a bully. She picks on kids who can't or won't defend themselves. She needs or likes the power she gets from putting others down. She might feel good about herself, or she might not. Bullies are not all alike. But what she definitely has is a need to control others, and she does it in mean, sneaky ways.

Why did Brenda become a bully? Perhaps she has been bullied by others—maybe by a parent or an older or bigger sibling. She feels powerless, so she builds her power by controlling others. Maybe she's jealous because Lauren is successful in school, something Brenda's not. Is it Lauren's fault that Brenda sought her out to bully? No way. Brenda's the one who's at fault, not Lauren. Lauren might have been picked on because she's shy or small or whatever—bullies can always find some reason for why they target a particular kid. If Lauren weren't available to bully, someone else would conveniently become the target.

Brenda is one kind of bully. She uses words to tease and control. Other bullies use fists or physical threats to feel powerful. They want to scare you and make you feel unsafe. Many girls won't admit that they've been bullied because they're embarrassed. But ignoring the situation won't make it go away.

Fighting Back

Whether the bullying is physical or not, when you're bullied you're going to feel angry. You might also feel scared or hurt. Maybe you even feel like crying.

How can you fight back against a bully? In a lot of different ways. And it's important to learn several strategies since the first one you try might not work or might not be the right one for the situation you're in. Or you might need to apply more than one technique to have an effect. Here are some ideas:

* Remember that the bully is wrong, not you. Don't let your self-esteem suffer when it's the bully who's behaving badly.
* Act self-confident. Bullies are less likely to pick on a girl who seems strong and sure of herself. When you're talking to a bully, practice your best posture, and talk in a loud, clear voice. You may be shaking inside, but if you act confident, the bully is more likely to walk away.
* Don't think you have to be polite. This is one situation where being rude may actually help you.
* If you are afraid that the bully will hurt you and other people are around, yell out something that will get someone's attention (perhaps "This boy is hurting me."). Girls have sometimes found themselves in dangerous situations, but the people who were nearby did nothing because they did not recognize that someone was in danger. So make it absolutely clear that you need help.
* Ask your friends to support you. If you have been bullied in the lunchroom, be sure to sit with a group and let them know who has been making your life miserable. A bully will have a harder time picking on someone who's surrounded by friends.
* Talk to an adult who can help—a parent, a teacher, the person in charge of the after-school activity where the bullying took place.
* Run if you find yourself in a situation that is immediately

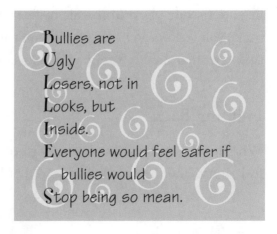

Bullies are
Ugly
Losers, not in
Looks, but
Inside.
Everyone would feel safer if
   bullies would
Stop being so mean.

threatening. Then report what happened to a parent or another adult who can take action.

If one of your friends is being bullied, how can you help her? Give her some advice—take whatever you want from the prior list. Agree with her that the bully is a jerk. If you're really brave—and only if the bully is not the physical type and you have your friend's permission—confront the bully yourself. Perhaps you can embarrass the bully into better behavior. Or let the bully know that there are better ways to get attention.

What If You're a Bully?

When you read Brenda's story, did it ring a bell? Did her behavior sound suspiciously like something you might have done? As is the case with harassment, once you recognize that you're doing something wrong, you've taken the most important step toward making a change in your life.

Do This: Figure out why you tease or bully others—what do you get out of it? What can you do instead to feel powerful and in control? You might get ideas from other sections of this book as well as

Liz Says:

Once in a while, my friends will tease me about my height (I'm short for my age) or about being quiet (yeah, I'm that, too). Someone might say, "Liz, you're making too much noise," when I actually haven't said a word. I'll answer with a friendly loud "Okay." When I make a joke about it and I don't let the situation bother me, it doesn't go any further. I know that bullying goes on in some places, but I'm lucky that there doesn't seem to be a whole lot of it at my school. But if I find myself face to face with a tough bully, I'll try to remember the tips in this book.

from an adult who can guide you as you learn to relate to others with greater respect. Never think that once a bully, always a bully. If you want to become someone who helps instead of remaining someone who hurts, make that your goal and start working on it right now.

Home Alone

Lots of kids your age spend time at home alone. While being home alone has made for some very funny movies, real life is a little different. Some girls like staying home alone—they feel independent and responsible, and they get to set and follow their own schedule. Others would prefer to have some company. Maybe they're afraid—they worry about all the things that could go wrong. Whether you're happy about staying alone or not, you may have no choice in the matter. Perhaps there's no adult or older sibling available after school to spend time with you and no after-school program conveniently located or affordable for your family. If you're going to be home alone, you might as well develop a positive attitude about it, learn some skills to help you stay safe, and find out about activities that you can do for fun.

Look at the following list and check the things that you know. Then find out how to do the ones that you didn't check. Make some notes to help you remember the most important details. You'll feel a whole lot more comfortable once you've checked everything on the list.

- ❏ How to change a fuse or reset the circuit breaker
- ❏ The emergency number in your community (often 911, but not always)
- ❏ The phone numbers of your parents at work
- ❏ How to turn off the water if a pipe bursts
- ❏ What to do if you smell gas
- ❏ The phone number of your nearest neighbor
- ❏ Who has an extra key if you accidentally get locked out of your house

❏ How to reach the superintendent of your building if you live in an apartment house

❏ What to do in a weather emergency, such as a hurricane, tornado, or lightning storm

❏ How to respond on the phone to a caller who asks for a parent or to someone who's at your door

For most of the items on the list, you'll have to enlist the help of a parent. But this next list gives some advice for dealing with the last one:

❀ Never let someone know you're home alone (or with just a friend or younger sibling).

❀ You might respond by saying, "My mom/dad is busy right now and can't come to the phone/door. May I have your name and telephone number so he/she can get back to you?" Write down messages so your parents won't miss anything important. If the person on the phone keeps calling back or the person at the door is insistent about coming into your house (perhaps the man in the delivery uniform says, "I have a package I must leave for your mom now. She said I should leave it with you."), call a parent if you can reach one of them or a neighbor for help. If you have not been able to get through to anyone or if the situation seems dangerous, call the police. Don't worry about being embarrassed later when you find out that your mom really did insist that the package be left but forgot to tell you. You used good judgment to stay safe, and she'll be proud of you. You should be proud of yourself, too.

Home Alone Can Be Fun

While the last section may make staying home alone seem a little scary, you could use the time to do some fun activities. Here are a few ideas that you can try—after you've completed your homework and chores and eaten a snack, of course!

* Make an art project that could be used as a gift. For example, you could decorate a plain wooden frame with buttons, shells, sequins, or beads. You might make a friendship bracelet with thread or yarn. Or you could try your hand at creating origami animals.

* Write a short play. With no distractions, you can concentrate on developing interesting characters and a plot.

* Write to a friend or relative who lives far away, or write a letter to the editor of your local paper about an issue that you've been thinking about.

* Surprise your family by preparing dinner or a special dessert (but only if you're allowed to).

* Choreograph a new dance routine or practice juggling.

Liz Says:

When I first started staying home alone after school, the first thing I would do is call my dad to let him know that I had arrived safely. Now, I only call if I have something I need to tell him. My mom and dad usually call just to say "hi," to find out if there's any interesting news, and sometimes to remind me to practice piano or get started on my homework. I don't mind being home alone—in fact, I like it. Being allowed to be on my own for a few hours makes me feel mature, responsible, and independent, and I get to play the music I like.

Good Decisions for Your Body—and Your Life

Recent studies have found that pre-teen girls are making decisions about activities and issues that, years ago, they probably would not have had to face until they became teens. Girls today at ten, eleven, and twelve are asking: "Should I diet to lose weight? What will boys think if I cut my hair? Should I start smoking? What should I do to get a boyfriend? Should I date a boy who is four years older than I am? Should I drink beer at a party?"

When you make positive decisions, you have collected the information you need and you've thought through the likely consequences. For instance, for the question "Should I diet to lose weight?" you might talk to your doctor about the proper weight range for your build and age (you're getting the information you need), and you might think about what you will look like and feel like at a lower weight (you're thinking about what will happen). Making good decisions means that you've probably thought through your choices ahead of time and come up with what you're going to say or do. Waiting until you get to a party where most kids are smoking or drinking or using drugs to decide what you will say is not smart decision making.

Making Decisions About Smoking

One important decision you may have already made or will make soon is about smoking. Answering these questions will tell you how likely you are to smoke:

Do you have close friends who smoke?   ❑ Yes ❑ No

Do you think that cigarettes make you look cool?   ❑ Yes ❑ No

Ask yourself these two questions every time you have to make an important decision: What do I need to know to make a good decision? What is likely to happen as a result of this decision?

Do you think smoking is a good way to lose weight or keep you slim?

     ❑ Yes ❑ No

Are you curious about cigarettes?

     ❑ Yes ❑ No

Does someone at home smoke?

     ❑ Yes ❑ No

Every yes answer you give to these questions increases your likelihood that you will smoke or that you're already a smoker. Does that mean that if you had three or more yes answers, you have no choice but to become addicted to tobacco? Definitely not. Understanding risk factors—those things or people that make you more likely to smoke—will help you make a positive decision. If you've already started smoking, you can make the decision to quit. But to be successful at giving up cigarettes, you may have to make some changes in your attitudes—from seeing smoking as cool to viewing it as an unhealthy, expensive habit, for example. And you'll have to really work at quitting since the nicotine in cigarettes is addictive, as you read in chapter 2. Ask a nonsmoking friend to support your efforts to quit smoking. And if you're not a smoker, but you have a friend who is, do that friend a life-saving favor—help him or her to give up tobacco.

Lots of girls are concerned about their parents who are smokers. You have probably already found out that you can't force them to give up this habit, but you can express your concerns. Since adults already know all about the terrible effects of tobacco, information alone is not going to have an effect. But you can support them when they try to quit.

What About Drinking?

Becoming aware of the special risks for girls of using alcohol—either while they're still developing or abusing it when they're older—can help you avoid making a serious mistake. Compared to boys, girls produce less of an enzyme in the body that helps digest alcohol. That means that less alcohol gets digested

Inhaling the smoke exhaled by smokers can make you sick. Studies have found that second-hand smoke can cause heart disease, lung cancer, and other serious illnesses.

and more alcohol reaches the bloodstream, causing girls to feel the effects of alcohol more quickly and with less of the drug (and yes, alcohol is a drug—a very powerful one).

Alcohol impairs how you think and make judgments and puts you at greater risk for behaving in ways you would never do while sober (and would regret later). That's why girls are more likely to have sex, including unprotected sex, if they've been drinking. They might start fights or get into a car with a driver who's been drinking. Making bad decisions is typical of people who have been drinking, since alcohol affects that part of the brain that allows them to be alert and aware. That's why someone who's been drinking may think that she can still drive—she has a false sense of confidence in her abilities.

Do This:

If you're ever in a position where someone who has been drinking offers to drive you somewhere (remember the situation described at the beginning of this chapter), find another way to get there. Call a parent or a taxi—don't get into a car with a person who's been drinking because you don't want to offend her. While you

Liz Says:

I'm lucky that no one in my family smokes, and I would never smoke. For a long time, my grandma smoked, but I didn't know about it until one day when my brother caught her sneaking a cigarette outside our house. It's funny that people usually talk about kids sneaking cigarettes, but here was my grandma doing it. Everyone tried to get her to stop smoking, but nothing worked until she became really ill, and the doctor said she absolutely had to stop smoking. I guess he scared her into quitting. Her breath smells a lot better now.

Q. *My parents drink. Why shouldn't I?*

A. Your parents are adults. As such, they can make the decisions about when and how to drink responsibly. That means that they understand the effect that alcohol has on their bodies. They recognize their limits and know when and where they can drink. Responsible drinkers would never drive after using alcohol. At your age, alcohol can impair your development. And, in most states, you're not allowed legally to drink until you're twenty-one. When you become an adult, you can make a decision about whether and when you're going to drink. If one of your parents has a problem with alcohol, you might want to share your concerns with a counselor or contact a group like Alateen, an organization that supports families and friends of alcoholics (1-800-344-2666).

Q. *Why do people who get drunk first seem happy and then act really sad?*

A. Alcohol is actually a depressant. It may give people a brief high, but that's followed by feeling down. People who drink to avoid facing problems find that their escape from reality is short-lived, and they're often left feeling even worse than they were before they drank. Depression and suicide attempts have been linked to the use of alcohol.

Q. *Do most kids drink?*

A. The simple answer is no. Surveys of middle school and high school students report that more kids don't drink than do. So if someone tries to convince you to drink because "everyone's doing it," you can answer, "That's just not true." And even if most kids were drinking, would that mean you should be doing it, too? You've probably already heard the following question (or a variation) from some adult in your life: "If everyone were jumping off the roof of a tall building (or a cliff or a bridge), would you go along and do it, too?" You know the answer to that question.

may have been trained to be polite, this is the situation that cries out to be the exception.

See the questions and answers on page 96. You may find these are questions you have about this topic:

What if you've already started drinking? Making one mistake, or even several, is never an excuse for making more of them. If you have already developed a drinking problem, you need to get help, and fast. Talk to a parent, your doctor, a school nurse, or someone else you trust who can make sure you get the help you need. And if you're hanging around with a group of friends who drink, you are probably better off finding a new group of friends. It's hard to keep saying no to peer pressure. When you're surrounded by kids who drink, that behavior may begin to seem normal or okay to you. But it's not. Think about your dreams and how drinking could make those dreams disappear right before your eyes.

Other Drugs

Perhaps now, but certainly as you get older, you will find yourself in situations in which other kids ask you to try marijuana or some other illegal drugs. You may be proud of yourself when you don't join them in doing drugs, but still find it hard to keep saying no. Here are some tips:

* ✿ Don't go to a party where you know drugs are likely to be available. If you find yourself in a social situation in which drugs are being used, leave. If you stay, be clear that you don't do drugs. If you sound hesitant when asked, you're more likely to be asked again. That hesitation might be taken as a sign that you could be convinced.
* ✿ Find and keep friends who don't use drugs, and promise that you'll support each other to stay away from drugs. If one of your friends starts using drugs, support her by helping her stop, not by agreeing to keep that information from her family.

✿ Get involved in activities like sports, writing, hiking, jogging, dancing, or volunteering that are fun and make you feel good about yourself.

Avoiding Sexual Involvement

Do you feel attracted to certain people? Do you have a crush on a famous sports star or musician or even someone you know, like a teacher? That's expected at your age. Having sexual feelings and thinking about what it would be like to have a sexual relationship with one of these people is normal. But acting on them by having sex is not. However, you might want to dance with a boy or hold hands with him, and that might feel really good to you. But don't say yes to a boy who wants you to dance or kiss or hold hands just because he asks. You don't even need to have a reason. You can just say, "No, I'm not interested." It's your body and you have a right to say no any time you want to. And even if you agreed to kiss someone one time doesn't give that person the right to demand that you kiss again at another time or on another day. Trust your instincts.

As you grow up, you will find that your sexuality is an important part of who you are. Exploring and sharing sexually with another person adds an exciting dimension to life, but it's an activity that requires maturity, knowledge, commitment, love, and trust—qualities that are part of being an adult. Preteens and teens are not in a position to accept the risks (like pregnancy or sexually transmitted diseases) and responsibilities that go along with having

Five Good Reasons to Stay Away from Cigarettes, Alcohol, and Other Drugs

1. They harm your health.

2. They ruin your reputation.

3. They hurt your relationship with your family.

4. They're expensive.

5. They destroy your future.

sex with a partner. A satisfying sexual relationship means waiting for the right person and the right time.

⟲ ⟲ ⟲

When an adult uses a kid for his or her own sexual pleasure, that's always wrong. Look back at situation 6 on page 82. If something like that has happened or ever happens to you, tell an adult who you trust, someone who can protect you and prevent it from happening again. If the person you told doesn't believe you or won't do anything about it, tell someone else. You deserve to stay safe.

You've already had the opportunity to make lots of decisions in your life. And you'll be making many more in the future. Practice asking good questions when you're faced with a dilemma and take the time to listen to both your mind and your heart. Each has a role to play in the choices you make. The more you learn at this age, the better prepared you'll be for the decisions and commitments you'll be making later on. And remember, some of the choices you make now can be life changing—for better or worse.

CHAPTER 5

Lessons in Learning

Making Your Time Count in and out of School

What kind of student are you? Do you study just enough to get by, or do you set high standards that you strive to reach? Who do you call a "good" teacher? Someone who doesn't demand much on tests or homework? You know, the type who gives an A for doing little more than writing your name on your test paper. Or is a good teacher someone who challenges you and makes you think? How do you fit your homework and study time into your day? Do you constantly feel rushed and behind in your work? Or have you figured out an effective way to manage everything you have to or want to do? Do you take on demanding projects in school to build your skills? Or do you usually choose the easiest assignments so you can get through the task quickly and go on to some other activities you'd rather do? This chapter is all about school—your homework, your teachers, your tests, your projects, your grades, and the way you organize your time to get all your work done.

What Kind of Student Are You?

You spend a lot of time in school taking quizzes and tests. And the grades should help you figure out how much you know and how much you don't.

But remember that grades are far from a perfect measure of your knowledge or ability. The quiz on page 103 will help you figure out just what kind of student you are. You won't get a grade, so breathe a sigh of relief. But you will find out about your learning style—how you learn best, how to improve your skills, and what kinds of situations to avoid.

Complete each sentence with the answer that best describes how you typically act or feel. You may not think any of the answers make sense for you or that more than one answer fits. However, do your best to select just one answer for each question, the one that comes closest to representing the real you. You might also want to put a mark next to the runner-up response. When it comes time to review what your answers mean, check out the choices that you almost picked as well as the ones you actually chose. That way, you'll learn a lot about the kind of student you are.

Talking About Teachers

As a student, you're bound to come across all kinds of teachers—the great, the good, the so-so, the bad, and the truly awful. That's preparation for the rest of your life. You're going to meet all kinds of people and have all kinds of bosses, coworkers, customers, even friends. Learning to get along with all types of people—whether you like them or not—is an important skill to have no matter what you do.

Who's your favorite teacher of all time? What makes him or her stand out? What qualities make a particular teacher stand head and shoulders above the crowd? Students say that great teachers have these qualities:

* **Help students achieve.** Easy teachers may have an awesome reputation, but students who are in their classes quickly learn that there's more to a good teacher than easy tests and little homework. Can you see the advantage of having a teacher who helps you achieve all that you're capable of?

Quiz: What Kind of Student Are You?

1. When I do my homework, I
   a. keep the radio on since the music helps me concentrate.
   b. must be alone in a quiet space.
   c. like to discuss my answers with friends or a family member.
   d. have to take breaks every few minutes since sitting for a long time makes me crazy.

2. If I have to take tests, I prefer those that
   a. are multiple-choice.
   b. allow me to write essays explaining my answers.
   c. just ask for the facts.
   d. encourage me to use my creativity.

3. I enjoy
   a. doing crossword puzzles and other word games.
   b. math problems more than word problems.
   c. problems where there is only one right answer.
   d. problems that can be answered in several different ways.

4. The subject I like the most is
   a. gym.
   b. music.
   c. language arts.
   d. computers.

5. When I work on projects, I
   a. enjoy making them look attractive.
   b. do a lot of research to make sure I have all the facts.
   c. spend huge amounts of time thinking before getting started.
   d. brainstorm with classmates or friends to get the best ideas.

(continues)

(continued from page 103)

6. When my teacher gives me a worksheet to complete, I
   a. know I'm going to be bored.
   b. feel relieved since I prefer those kind of straightforward assignments.
   c. know I won't have to spend much time on it.
   d. wish I could trade it in for a project that lets me be more creative.

7. I usually receive my highest grades in
   a. math.
   b. art.
   c. social studies.
   d. all my subjects.

8. When it's time for my teacher to check our notebooks, I
   a. cringe—mine is always a disorganized mess.
   b. am prepared—mine is usually neat and organized.
   c. wonder what he/she will think about the cartoon characters that fill the pages.
   d. hope he/she won't be able to read the private little notes I've written for myself.

9. I love using the gym
   a. when it's taken over by the yearly book fair.
   b. to play team sports.
   c. to work on my rope-climbing skills.
   d. to show off my science fair project.

10. When the school year starts, I can't wait
    a. to get my new school supplies.
    b. to see my friends at lunch.
    c. to find out what books we'll be reading.
    d. to learn a new language.

What do your answers mean?

1. Doing Your Homework
   a. Music helps you work, rather than distracting you. But if you find yourself singing out loud to most of the songs, then you're probably paying more attention to music than to math, and you might want to turn off the sound for a while. In fact, if you're working on a really difficult problem, music probably prevents you from giving 100 percent of your brain power to finding a solution. Get the work done first and enjoy the music later.
   b. While you probably enjoy the company of friends, you've learned from experience that you concentrate best when you're not distracted—by conversation, music, or noise.
   c. You're a people person when it comes to learning. The give and take of group problem solving works for you. Just know that from time to time, like when you're in school facing a test, you won't be able to depend on brainstorming with friends to find answers. So it's best to get some practice working on your own.
   d. Sitting in one place drives you crazy, so reward yourself each time you complete two math problems or learn five new spelling words. Have a jump rope handy, juggle some balls, or do a few sit-ups—anything that moves your body. Then get right back to work before you've forgotten what the homework's all about.

2. Taking Tests
   a. If you prefer multiple-choice tests, either you like the structure or you haven't learned the material well enough to write about it without the clues. The next time you study, ask yourself some questions, or have a family member do so, and practice answering them. You'll feel more prepared for your next test, and you'll have a better handle on the material.

(continues)

(continued from page 105)

    b. If you prefer to write out your answers, you probably feel comfortable with words and with explaining information.

    c. You're good at memorizing facts. You might want to work on gaining a deeper understanding of what you're learning—why and how something happened.

    d. You're not afraid of a challenge, and you recognize that there's often more than one way to arrive at an answer.

3. Solving Problems

    a. You're good with words, an important skill in all types of subjects. Be sure to work on your math skills, too, since you'll need those to succeed.

    b. You're good with numbers, which is great, since they're important in solving lots of problems and many jobs rely on your math ability. However, don't neglect your reading, since that's a lifelong skill as well.

    c. You feel most comfortable with the kind of problem that has only one answer. But lots of problems can be solved in a variety of ways. Get some experience in endeavors that allow you to explore your creative side—perhaps painting a scene or writing song lyrics.

    d. You like to use your creativity. You may need to help your teachers understand that sometimes there really is more than one right answer.

4. Enjoying School

    a. If gym is your favorite subject, maybe it's because you're bored sitting for an extended period of time. In your regular classes, volunteer to do blackboard work, run an errand, work with another student—anything that allows you to get up for a short time. You'll be able to concentrate better when you get back to your seat.

    b. Hello, music fan! Use your interest in music to increase your knowledge of other subjects. Compose a new piece of music—

use your math skills to work out the pattern and tempo. Read about women who compose or conduct.

   c. If language arts is a favorite subject, you probably spend a lot of time exploring through books. Look for library books that are different from your usual fare. If you're always reading mysteries, try biographies. If you usually head right to the fiction section, looking for stories about today's girls, or check out a historical novel or two for a change.

   d. Your interest in computers is a real plus in today's world. Every field, from fashion design to engineering, relies on computers. With your friends, explore exciting new software and hardware—there's so much to learn and do.

5. Working on Projects
   a. It's great to be interested in art and to make projects look good, but be sure there's substance behind the looks. As is true of people, projects need to be good, not just good-looking.

   b. It's important to look up facts and to record them accurately. But don't become a perfectionist, someone who needs to work on a project until it is flawless. Perfectionists never feel satisfied with what they've done and just keep working on and on and on. . . .

   c. Taking some time to think before starting a project is a good strategy. You will avoid problems later on. What you need to watch for is thinking for so long and so hard that you don't give yourself enough time for the doing.

   d. Brainstorming with others is often a useful way to gather ideas. Just be sure that being with friends doesn't become the primary reason for getting together.

6. Completing Worksheets
   a. While you know from past experience that worksheets bore you, try to get something out of every assignment. An open mind will allow you to learn something.

(continued from page 107)

b. You probably feel comfortable with worksheets since they're not likely to tax your mind. To extend your learning, look for assignments that are a bit more stimulating.

c. You're confident about your knowledge. Now think about what you're going to do with the time you've saved by doing the work so quickly.

d. Not every assignment is going to allow you to use your creative energy. Your teacher will appreciate your cooperation when you do your worksheet. Perhaps she'll remember that when you suggest a different kind of assignment the following week.

7. Getting High Grades

a. You don't listen to stereotypes about boys doing well in math and girls receiving high grades in reading. Hurray for you— you're your own person. Now, stay that way.

b. Use your artistic touch to brighten up your reports, and your teachers may notice that you have other talents as well.

c. Doing well in social studies means that you understand the lessons of history. See whether you can apply them to your own life.

d. You're smart enough to know that being a good student is not a bad thing. In fact, knowing how to learn prepares you for later success.

8. Checking Out Notebooks

a. You might be able to fool some people when you say, "A disorganized notebook is a sign of genius," but your teacher's probably not going to be one of them.

b. As long as you're not becoming compulsive about it, keeping your school papers organized makes it easier to get your work done—and find permission slips for trips.

c. If your teacher has any kind of sense of humor and you're doing well in school, he or she will appreciate the fine art in your notebook. Besides, doodling is less disruptive than talking.

d. Instead of hoping your teacher won't be able to read the notes, cross them out as quickly and thoroughly as possible. Perhaps you can find a better way to communicate in the future. Your teacher is probably less interested in the content of your private notes than in how well you're doing in class.

9. Working Out or Not
   a. It's wonderful to love reading, but make sure you take advantage of opportunities to train your body as well as your mind.
   b. Team sports not only teach specific athletic skills but also build your self-confidence and prepare you for the people-to-people situations you'll find yourself in throughout your life.
   c. Go, girl! Show them how strong you are.
   d. Studying science is cool, but don't feed into the stereotype of the scientist locked away in a lab oblivious to the world. Use the gym for working out and releasing tension.

10. Beginning the School Year
    a. The new school year is an opportunity not just to get new school supplies but to start fresh. Discard old habits that didn't work for you, and learn some new ones that will lead you right to success.
    b. Yes, friends are a critical part of school life, but try to keep learning your number one priority. You have plenty of time after school, on weekends and holidays, and during vacation for hanging out with your buds.
    c. Expand your book list this year to something a little different—something you've rarely tried before—perhaps biographies, mysteries, historical fiction, short stories.
    d. Being excited about learning a new language means that you're open to different cultures and ways of thinking and doing. Share that attitude with peers who may not be as open as you are.

❋ **Are fair.** Fair teachers assign a reasonable amount of homework and give tests on material either covered in class or from assigned material in the textbook (but avoid asking questions about the information found in a tiny footnote or the caption under a picture). Here's an example of a fair teacher: After most of the students failed their social studies test (it was given the morning after an unexpected hurricane hit town), Ms. Brown allowed everyone to retake the test. The students who received high grades the first time around did not have to take the test but were given extra credit. The teacher favored neither the students who did well nor the ones who did poorly. She was fair to the whole class.

❋ **Are trustworthy.** How would you feel if you told your teacher something very personal to explain why you hadn't finished your homework, and then she revealed what you said as an example in class? She didn't refer to you by name, but you and everyone else could easily figure out that you were the subject of the example. If this happened to you, you'd probably feel betrayed, angry, and humiliated. As for your future relationship with this teacher—well, it's hard to learn from a teacher you don't trust or respect.

❋ **Make learning fun.** Funny stories help students remember facts, and jokes relieve tension. Learning is serious business, but good teachers know that a classroom doesn't have to be serious all the time for students to learn.

Teachers like students who are

- Curious. They want to know more; they challenge in a respectful way.
- Team players. They cooperate with teachers and with other students.
- Energetic and enthusiastic learners. They come to school prepared to learn, with books, papers, pens, pencils, and an open mind.

If you have teachers who are funny or interesting, let them know that you appreciate the extra effort they put into their work to make learning fun for everyone. Everyone likes to hear a compliment, and teachers are no exception. If you feel awkward about expressing your appreciation face to

Liz Says:

I've learned that every new school year is totally different from the ones that came before. Over the summer in between sixth and seventh grades, I thought that school would be basically the same and that I would get used to it quickly. But that wasn't the case. I did get used to school, but I found that lots of things were different, not necessarily better or worse, just different. I had totally new teachers, and, for the first time, I was learning a foreign language—Spanish. And to make things more complicated, that subject was taught in a math classroom. When I got there the first day, I almost left thinking I had to be in the wrong place since all I could see were math symbols and numbers on posters around the room and French words on the board. (There's a French class in that room right before I get there for Spanish.)

This year my last class of the day is in a room that is nowhere near my locker, so I had to get used to rushing there and still getting to the bus before it left. At some point, I realized that school this year wasn't what I'd expected—some classes were harder, or easier, than I thought they'd be, and some of what I had heard about my teachers was different from the way they turned out to be—and not necessarily in a bad way. So each school year is going to be different from what you expect. Just stay cool, and you'll eventually get used to it.

face, do it in a card. Thanksgiving Day is a good time to tell a teacher how grateful you are.

* **Control the classroom.** Few students want a very strict, inflexible teacher, but most would like the classroom to be quiet enough to hear what's going on. A dozen loud conversations going on at the same time, paper airplanes and assorted other objects flying across the room, and kids jumping out of their seats add up to a funny sitcom on TV. But that kind of atmosphere would probably not be so funny in real life. How can you, as just one student, contribute to a classroom atmosphere that works?

* **Are knowledgeable.** You might like having a nice teacher, but it's essential to have a teacher who knows the subject. Paying attention pays off in this kind of classroom.

* **Want to make a difference in their students' lives.** Ask your parents or other adults about a teacher who made a difference in their lives. If the question unleashes a flood of vivid memories, you know that the teacher had a big impact. Great teachers can do that. If you haven't already had such a teacher, maybe you'll be lucky enough next year or the year after to get one of those teachers—someone who cares about you, wants you to learn, and inspires you to be your best.

Do This: In the space on page 113 or in your journal, describe either your favorite teacher or an ideal teacher. You might also want to write about a teacher to whom you would not give a very good report card grade. Anything you can do to help this teacher make the grade?

What's So Important About Math and Science?

You've probably heard at least one teacher, and maybe a parent or another relative, tell you how important it is for girls to stay interested in math and

My Favorite or Ideal Teacher

_____

_____

_____

_____

_____

_____

_____

_____

_____

_____

_____

_____

_____

_____

_____

_____

_____

_____

_____

_____

_____

_____

science. If you haven't, here's your chance to hear it. And if you have heard the message, have you been listening?

Most girls start out in elementary school doing really well in math and science. But at some point, some of them decide that they're not good in those subjects or that those subjects aren't important or interesting. Why the change of heart? For some, it's because their moms and other female adults shy away from math and science—probably because they didn't have very positive experiences when they were younger. And, as girls get older, some of them receive the message (from books or people or movies) that these subjects are more important or more interesting for boys than for girls. That's

Liz Says:

Here's a funny way to keep your sense of humor when thinking about teachers. Ask one of your friends to give you a word to fill in each of the parentheses in the following paragraph (but don't let her see the paragraph before she's given all her answers). While your teachers might not appreciate the hilarity of the completed paragraph, they might be glad that you and your friend are getting a lesson in parts of speech. Read the paragraph aloud to your friend so you can both get a good laugh.

About My Teacher

I once had a teacher who was (number) years old and quite (adjective). She taught (a school subject), but she was not very (adjective). One day while she was teaching her class, (name) started to (verb) very (adverb). My teacher then (verb in the past tense) and the whole class started to (verb). My teacher was (a feeling) and then left the (type of room). Now she just eats (plural noun) and (verb).

An Alphabet for Learning

Ask questions—you won't look silly; you're being smart.

Bring your supplies to school and be prepared to work.

Challenge yourself—don't take the easy way out.

Do some homework every night—don't let it pile up.

Expect to do well—and you're more likely to.

Find a quiet spot to think.

Gather what you need before you begin to study.

Help other students and you'll learn, too.

Ignore distractions—and don't use them as excuses for not studying.

Joke around, but don't get carried away.

Keep your school stuff in one place so you don't waste time looking for missing things.

Learn as much as you can in school—and out.

Make studying a priority in your life.

Notice what's on the blackboard: Test dates? Homework assignments?

Organize your notebooks and workspace.

Participate in class

Question your teacher when you don't understand.

Reach for your dreams.

Show others what you know.

Tell your teacher when you need to know more.

Understand what you've read before you move on.

Visit libraries and museums—remember that learning takes place outside the school building, too.

Watch TV after your homework's done.

X out activities that interfere with learning.

Yearn to learn—and grow.

Zero in on what's really important.

absolutely *not true*. No matter what career you pursue or what you do with your life, these subjects will play a key role. Take a closer look.

Do This:

For the next twenty-four hours, keep a diary or use table 5-1 to keep track of when and how you use math and science (see example in the table). Obviously, you shouldn't set your alarm to wake you through the night (although if you did so, you would be using math and perhaps a computer—depending on the kind of clock you have). But during your waking hours—in school, at home, in stores, at your after-school activities—check out how much of your life is tied to math and science. Remember to think about math and science in broad terms. Solving a problem might be math or science or both. Cooking involves math and science—you do have to measure ingredients, don't you? Or double a recipe because you need cupcakes for sixteen, not just eight. Butter melts when it is heated—science, right? What happens to the sugar crystals that dissolve into the water? Isn't that a science question? And these questions are just about cooking. What about shopping? (You make change.) Exercising? (You can track heart rate changes.) Scheduling your time? (You figure out how much time you have to do your homework in between your dance class and dinner.) Taking shelter during a lightning storm? (You know that lightning is electrical so it's smart to stay away from metal and tall objects, like trees.) You get the point.

See if you can get a friend or a family member—maybe someone who claims not to like or be good at science or math—to do this diary activity, too. Or maybe you can convince your teacher that this would be an interesting homework assignment for the class. It might be fun to compare notes with other people to see the similarities and differences in your diaries and in your answers to the questions on page 119.

After you have completed your twenty-four-hour math/science diary, ask yourself the questions on page 119:

Table 5-1. Math & Science Log

Time	How you used science and math
7:00 a.m.	Alarm clock indicated the time.

(continues)

(continued from page 117)

Table 5-1. Math & Science Log

Time	How you used science and math

Math and Science
Learning Questions

1. How much of your day is spent with math or science?
2. Where are you most likely to use math and science?
3. What surprised you most?
4. What did you learn about yourself? About the role math and science play in your life?

When you get to chapter 8, you'll have a chance to find out more about science and math in careers and the role of computers in your life now and in the future.

Challenge Yourself

It's always tempting to choose the easiest assignment when you have a choice (perhaps you fall back on the tried and true science fair project rather than investigating something new and different—and harder to complete). Or you write the least number of sentences in a composition (your teacher requires at least ten sentences so you give her exactly ten). What's the advantage of trying

Liz Says:

I don't really like school science that much, but I do like hands-on science. In school we do experiments, and we do get some time to work with science materials, but then you have to write a lab report about it and fill out sheets, and it isn't fun anymore. As a Girl Scout, I've done some fun science like cleaning up after an oil spill to find out what works. Of course, this was not in a real river or ocean but in a small basin where a feather represented a bird, a fake fur piece stood for an animal, and a cup of sand stood for an entire beach. We got so involved in this project that one of my friends took the fake fur piece home and carried it around for a while as if it were a pet.

As for math, I like math because I'm good at it. I get good grades in math even though it's not always particularly fun. I do like the challenge of solving math problems.

something a little harder or with more risk? You'll learn a little more and you'll gain skills and knowledge in new areas.

You don't have to wait for your teacher to come up with a challenging project for you to work on. You may be able to use one to satisfy a class requirement. But that's not really the point of these suggestions. Try one of these to stretch your mind:

* ♣ Create a board game for four or more players. Type up the directions so everyone can read them. Try to predict the questions that players will have and answer them in your directions for play. Design and construct the pieces, cards, board (which can be any size or shape), and anything else that's needed for your game. Some possible themes are famous women, endangered animals, travel in outer space, or food around the world. Use your imagination to come up with other possibilities.
* ♣ Invent something that can be used to save time or space or money. Develop the real object or create a model on paper. Half of the learning and fun will be deciding what you're going to invent.
* ♣ Write a book report or a book review for a book that exists only in your own mind. Create an author (with an interesting life) and a publishing company. Share the report with others to see whether what you wrote is believable. But stop them before they go crazy trying to order the book online.

What If You Hate School?

Maybe you wanted to skip this chapter because school is the last subject you wanted to read about. It's bad enough you have to go there every day. You're not concerned about finding enough challenge in school assignments. Your challenge is getting through the weeks and months between school vacations.

The only reason you're looking at this chapter at all is because the title of this section caught your eye. Now what?

This section is designed to help you figure out what you and your family can do to make your school experience a better one. First, figure out why you hate school. Is it because of a particular teacher? Because you're not doing well? Because you have a learning disability? Because you're being bullied? Because you have no friends at school? Is it a combination of these? Why is it important to identify what's going on? Because what you do will depend on why you're so miserable at school.

The second step is taking some kind of action. Here are some ideas for each of the situations just described:

Situation 1: You can't stand your teacher. Maybe she picks on you or other kids. She's nasty and yells a lot. Are you the only one who's having trouble with this teacher, or is your entire class upset? If the whole class is having a problem with the teacher, then some kind of group effort is needed, and you can help to lead it. Make an appointment to speak to the teacher (as a group), if she's the type to allow that. Prepare the points your group will make ahead of time. Make sure there's agreement among the students about the issues. The last thing you want is an argument in front of this teacher about what the problems are. If speaking is out of the question, write a group letter signed by everyone or as many classmates as you can get to do this. If you're alone in how you feel, you're going to have to deal with this situation with the help of a parent or on your own. But follow the same actions described already. What if the teacher refuses to meet with you or he or she meets with you, but the situation in class remains as awful as before—what next? You've been fair to your teacher by trying to work out the situation with him or her first. You may need to visit or write a letter to the principal next. Having the advice and support of a parent would be very helpful here.

Situation 2:

You used to do well in school, but now your grades are terrible. You dread going to school since almost every day you either take a test or get one returned to you—always with poor grades. What can you do? You need to figure out how this year is different from last year. Can you see the blackboard well enough? Can you clearly hear what the teacher is saying? Are you having trouble with math or reading? The answer might be as simple as getting glasses. Or you might need to study more than you used to since the material is getting more difficult. Perhaps you've developed a serious case of test anxiety. That means that you get so nervous when it's time to take a test that you can't think clearly. If that's your problem, talk to a teacher or school counselor or parent who can help you get over the fears that are preventing you from doing as well on tests as you're capable of.

Situation 3:

You've recently been told by your school psychologist that you have a learning disability. While you might want to use that as an excuse for doing poorly in school, don't! Maybe you do have more difficulty learning than some of your classmates do, but that doesn't mean you should just give up. Who benefits from giving up? Definitely not you! Find out how you can best learn and take tests. Talk to your teacher, parents, school psychologist, or reading specialist—lots of people probably want to help you. You may need to listen to books on tape, or get more time to take tests, or work with a tutor who can help you figure out some effective learning strategies. Even if you have not done well in school for a long time, try not to think that you will never do better. That kind of attitude is just going to stand in the way of your future success.

Situation 4:

You've just moved to a new community, and the school bully has decided that you would make a perfect target for nasty comments, a little push here or there, or some absolutely untrue but deliciously juicy gossip about your family. You never know when you walk into class what the other kids have heard, or what's going to happen to you as you make your way up the stairs from lunch, or why a group of students are whispering and laughing as they look in your direction. Going to school has become a miserable experience, and it has nothing to do with your teachers, your tests, or your grades. A bully has made you a victim because you're new at school and you haven't had time yet to surround yourself with supportive friends. If you haven't already read chapter 4 or if you have but you don't remember all the tips on dealing with bullies, turn to that section right now. Decide what action you're going to take and who's going to help you. You can't just ignore the bully, hoping he or she is going to fade away. While you're waiting, your schoolwork is suffering and so are you. You deserve better.

Situation 5: Your best friend—the one who's been by your side since you were a toddler—just moved to a far-away town. Another close friend has changed so much, becoming someone you don't know any longer and don't want to know. A third friend still lives in your neighborhood, but now she goes to a private school, and the two of you have totally different schedules. You don't even have the same school vacations. At lunch, you sit by yourself, and when your teacher assigns group projects, no one readily jumps up to join you. It's not bad when you're home—you have lots of hobbies and interests. But it's really tough for you in school—sitting by yourself at lunch, having to wait for the teacher to get you a partner for a class project, and walking home alone from school. What can you do to remedy this situation? If this is the first time you've had this problem, think about what you did before to make and keep friends. Put into practice some of those tried and true techniques, like being friendly (a smile and a cheerful greeting often go a long way) and interested in what others are talking about.

When you do get a partner for a school project, make the most of this opportunity. Ask your partner to come over to your house to work, and then combine work with fun. Do your share on the project so she'll want to work with you again. So will other kids.

What if you've always had trouble making friends? Do you think it's too late to start some new friendships? Absolutely *not!* What you need to do is figure out—with help from a parent, an older sibling, or another relative—what you're doing or not doing right. Be prepared for some honest answers from the people you ask. If you don't really want to hear constructive criticism, don't even bother asking the question. But then you'll continue to be a solo eater at lunch. You might be shy, but lots of shy kids have friends. You might think you don't have much in common with other kids, but how do you know if you haven't gotten to know them? If you attend a large school, you have the advantage of having lots of kids you might choose as friends, and many who might select you. But the downside is that you might not get noticed in the crowd. If you attend a school with a small number of kids—maybe a hundred or less—someone is bound to notice that you're alone most of the time and will seek you out—if you're open to a friendship, that is. But with a small number of students, you may not be able to be as picky, trying to find someone who's exactly like your friend who moved away. Besides, it's better to start fresh with someone different.

Whatever the particular situation you're in, work out a solution—with help from people who care about you—that's right for you and your circumstances. The one thing you shouldn't do is just continue to count the days until vacation.

Around the Clock

One of your biggest challenges in school and out is making the time for everything you want or need to do. It sounds corny, but learning to manage your time well is time well spent. Sometimes, you probably feel overwhelmed with your homework, friends, household chores, sports practices, and whatever else fills your days and nights. At other times you might wander around your house, complaining that you have nothing to do. Managing your time well lessens the stress from having too much to do and reduces the number of times you're bored to death.

Right now, your life may be pretty complicated. Answer the questions on page 126 with a simple yes or no answer.

Liz Says:

I've never actually hated school, but like every other student, I've had days when I wish I could have stayed at home. But I have a friend who dreads going to her math class every single day. Her teacher always picks on her and she says that "he's out to ruin her life." For instance, he always checks her homework, but for other students, he only checks their homework once in a while. So, of course, on the one day my friend forgot to do her homework, he announced to the whole class that he was going to call her mother at work. She was extremely embarrassed and mad at the teacher since she knew that her mom's boss would get angry about getting a personal phone call that was not an emergency. From that day on, my friend hated that teacher and the class even more. He was so mean to her that he lowered her grade to a C+, even though it averaged to a B. I guess if most teachers were like that, everyone would hate school. Fortunately, most teachers are better than that.

Do you have music or dance lessons?	❏ Yes	❏ No
Are you on a sports team?	❏ Yes	❏ No
Do you go for after-school help?	❏ Yes	❏ No
Do you have friends you like to e-mail?	❏ Yes	❏ No
Do you like to read or have one or more other hobbies?	❏ Yes	❏ No
Do you get homework almost every night?	❏ Yes	❏ No
Does your teacher sometimes assign long-term projects?	❏ Yes	❏ No
Are you expected to do chores at home?	❏ Yes	❏ No
Does your family have some together times— when everyone is supposed to be present?	❏ Yes	❏ No
Is spending time with friends important to you?	❏ Yes	❏ No
Do you visit relatives from time to time?	❏ Yes	❏ No
Do you spend some time as a volunteer, helping other people?	❏ Yes	❏ No
Are you expected to care for a younger sibling sometimes?	❏ Yes	❏ No

All of these questions point to activities and people that take up time. Some of the time is spent doing stuff that is really fun, and much of it is probably worthwhile or important. Even if you successfully manage the various aspects of your life now, what would happen if one more chore or activity or friend or whatever were tossed onto your list? It's time to develop some time management skills.

Use table 5-2 on one school day and one weekend day to track how you spend your time. Before you actually fill in the boxes, predict what you're going to find. After you've completed the chart, ask yourself these questions:

> Whatever you do as you get older, whether you become a forest ranger or an actress, a veterinarian or a business owner, you're going to need time management tools.

Table 5-2. How I Spend My Time

	School Day	Weekend Day
7:00 A.M.		
7:30 A.M.		
8:00 A.M.		
8:30 A.M.		
9:00 A.M.		
9:30 A.M.		
10:00 A.M.		
10:30 A.M.		
11:00 A.M.		
11:30 A.M.		
12:00 P.M.		
12:30 P.M.		
1:00 P.M.		
1:30 P.M.		
2:00 P.M.		
2:30 P.M.		
3:00 P.M.		
3:30 P.M.		
4:00 P.M.		
4:30 P.M.		

(continues)

(continued from page 127)

Table 5-2. How I Spend My Time

	School Day	Weekend Day
5:00 P.M.		
5:30 P.M.		
6:00 P.M.		
6:30 P.M.		
7:00 P.M.		
7:30 P.M.		
8:00 P.M.		
8:30 P.M.		
9:00 P.M.		
9:30 P.M.		
10:00 P.M.		

What did you learn about how you spend your time?

What surprised you most?

What seems to be your biggest time waster?

What are you going to do differently now that you know how you spend your time?

One of the actions you might take is to start a To Do list for the week. Use the format in table 5-3, which you can copy, or create a chart on a computer. As you complete items on your list, cross them out. At the end of the week, start a new list. Before you transfer leftover items onto the next week's list, ask yourself whether you really need to do this activity. If you find that you're shifting the same item from one week's To Do list to the next for a month or more,

Table 5-3. To Do Chart

Date Due	To Do for School	To Do for Home	To Do for Family	To Do for Friends	To Do for Hobbies	To Do Other

Liz Says:

I'm not a very scheduled person, and I tend to do things at the last minute. But then I feel stressed a few days before a project or report is due, wondering if I'll be able to complete the project and how much sleep I'll be getting the night before it's due. And I'm not the kind of person who does well with very little sleep. Sometimes when I don't have anything due the next day, I'll just relax after school instead of getting started on homework that's supposed to be finished the day after. Of course, the next day I find that I have tons of things to do and practically no time to get them done. I am really trying to develop better work habits since I've got lots of school years in front of me. I don't think I'll ever be able to schedule everything, and I don't think I want to, but waiting until the last minute to do everything is just too stressful.

eliminate that item once and for all by either doing it or crossing it out undone.

❧ ❧ ❧

You have a lot of years of schooling left in your life, particularly if you want to become a doctor or lawyer or scientist or professor. Even if those careers do not interest you now, who knows what will spur your interest in five, ten, or fifteen years. So figure out how to make the most of your school experiences and keep those lessons in learning with you for many years to come. And if you prefer not to look too far into the future, just think about how good you'll feel when you— and no one else in your family— know the answer to a question that's been asked on a popular TV game show. Too bad the million-dollar prize can't be given to an at-home contestant!

CHAPTER 6

Make It Happen in Your Community

Taking Action and Making a Difference

Every neighborhood or community has its very own personality, just as people do. Would you describe your town as friendly and open to newcomers or as a bunch of snobs who only trust those who've lived there forever? Is your town exciting with plenty of activities for kids and grownups? Or do you and most of your friends often complain that there's nothing to do? Do you live in a place with people from lots of different backgrounds, or are most of your neighbors pretty much clones of each other?

In the space provided in figures 1 and 2, capture the personality of your community in an abstract drawing—not with the actual buildings and streets, but with lines, shapes, and symbols that represent how you see the place where you live.

Example: If your town seems divided into two distinctly different groups who rarely play, work, or go to school together, you might draw a picture with a group of identical symbols on the left side of the page with a thick line down the center and a different set of identical symbols on the right side.

6 6 6

After you have completed your "My Community Now" drawing, do another one to represent how you would like your community to change. What do your drawings tell you?

Maybe you've always lived in the same town or city. Or perhaps you're part of a family that moves constantly. Wherever you are on the spectrum that

Figure 1. My Community Now

runs from staying put in one place all the way to always on the go, you're an important part of your community. And your community needs you!

This chapter will help you get to know and enjoy the place where you live and will give you some ideas for making it even better. Why should you get involved? For two very good reasons: It's the right thing to do for your community, and it will help you grow in more ways than you might imagine— meeting new people and finding out more about the ones you already know,

Figure 2. My Community As It Could Be

exploring hobbies and careers, doing something exciting and important, and discovering more about yourself.

What Needs to Get Done in Your Community?

When you live in a place for even a little while, you get so accustomed to your surroundings that you stop seeing them clearly. The homeless woman who pushes her shopping cart—crammed tight with her belongings stuffed into plastic grocery bags—up and down Main Street was very noticeable when you first moved in, but now she's become all but invisible. The families that wait in line at a soup kitchen to get a hot meal are still there even when no one bothers to see them.

Sometimes, a town is so overwhelmed by problems that it's easiest just to turn away from them, not to do anything. But if you attack just one small part of a problem, you make an important difference. And think about what would happen if lots and lots of girls, like you, decided that they were going to take some kind of action—even a small one—to make a difference in their communities. Big challenges can get broken down into little problems. These smaller problems are made up of individuals and

Liz Says:

Every person has a different reason for doing community service. Some people do it because they know that the people they help will appreciate it very much. I've seen the grateful expressions on faces at the nursing home where I've played piano or danced or given out cards or gifts. When you volunteer, you might make some new friends or just have more time to spend with kids you're already friends with. Helping others will definitely make you feel good about yourself, and you will probably have a whole lot of fun, too.

families who need help. And finally, people like you give their time, and sometimes supplies, food, clothing, or money, to change lives. So if you think there's no point in getting involved, think again. Your actions can have an important impact.

Preparing for Action

Before you take even a single step, learn as much as you can about what's going on in your town or city. Are there some very obvious needs? Perhaps you've read in the local newspaper that a group home for people who are mentally retarded is being built, and many neighbors are violently opposed to its construction. You would like to help people understand that those who are a little slow or who learn in a different way are just as entitled to live in a real home in a real community as anyone else. You have decided that your issue is welcoming group homes for individuals with developmental disabilities into your community. But you still have lots of work to do—to truly understand where negative attitudes come from and what the best strategies are for changing minds. But you've made an important first step. You have identified an issue that means something to you.

Reading local newspapers is one way to learn about what's happening in your community. How else can you gather the facts? You could listen to the news stories on the radio or on TV, or you could find out what's going on by reviewing the latest current events bulletins online. You could talk to the adults and kids in your family about what they think needs to be done. You might even create a short survey that you can give to a number of neighbors, friends, relatives, shop owners and workers, teachers, and other students, asking them to help you identify the needs of your community.

See page 136 for an example of a survey that you can use or adapt so it works for you. You could ask people to write in their answers, or you could obtain responses through a face-to-face or telephone interview. E-mail is another effective way to get answers. Lots of people who don't have time to respond in other ways are willing to jot down some quick answers online. The answers will give you a pretty good indication of the variety of issues you could work on and maybe even teach you about an issue you hadn't thought about at all. Before you give the survey to anyone else to answer, take it yourself. After all, your opinion is the most important one since you're the one who's going to take action.

What Needs to Happen in Our Community?

1. What do you think is the number one problem in our community?

   _____

2. What are the obstacles to dealing with this problem?

   _____

3. What organizations are now working on this issue?

   _____

4. What actions or strategies do you think could be effective in dealing with this problem?

   _____

5. Do you know people—adults or kids—who are interested in doing something about this issue? How can they be contacted?

   _____

6. What other serious problems or issues face our community today?

   _____

Once you've done your research and thought about the possible causes to get involved in, it's time to identify the specific issue you're going to tackle. But if you're still having trouble making a decision, use the eight questions on page 137 and look at the list of community issues on page 138 to narrow down your options.

What Do You Want to Do?

1. Are you more interested in helping younger kids, kids your own age, families, or animals?

   _____

2. What skills do you want to use in your volunteer work?

   _____

3. Do you prefer to do something as part of an after-school program, or do you want to work with an agency in your community?

   _____

4. Are you interested in starting something new or joining a program already in progress?

   _____

5. What one issue do you care about more than any other?

   _____

6. How much time do you have each week or each month to do volunteer work?

   _____

7. Do you want your community work to be related to one of your hobbies? If yes, which hobby might you work into volunteer service?

   _____

8. Are you interested in volunteering for an organization that will allow you to explore a career that intrigues you? If yes, what careers might be related to potential volunteer work?

   _____

Who Can You Work With?

Having a real impact in your community requires a lot of work. While you may have heard about instances of kids who made a difference in their community single-handedly, almost always, kids have had some help from others who were interested in the same causes. Maybe their parents helped them develop a plan or a teacher guided them through the rules and required permission forms (this kind of stuff is often called "red tape") at school, or friends created flyers publicizing their efforts, or siblings did record keeping, or cousins worked with them on fund-raising. No matter how motivated and strong and capable you are, you're probably better off finding other people who want to work with you than trying to do everything solo. You can take the lead, but other people can support you and probably help you to accomplish more than you would on your own. Another important advantage of working with others is that you're likely to have fun doing something together!

Working with a Group

Do you belong to or can you join a group, such as Girl Scouts, that often acts together to serve the community? It's often easiest to work with others who have similar interests. If you're not a Girl Scout, perhaps a friend who is a member can tell you about the kinds of volunteer work her group is involved in. If you're already a Girl Scout, try to interest other girls in your troop in planning and carrying out a service

Examples of Community Issues

Animal care
Conservation of natural resources
Recycling
Homeless people
Senior citizens
Abandoned animals
Recreation opportunities for pre-teens and teens
Literacy
Crime
Hunger and poverty
Use of car seat belts
After-school care for kids
Child abuse
Places to play sports
Substance abuse
Prejudice and discrimination
Kids with special needs
Traffic lights or signs
Homework help
Water quality
School safety

project together. Check out the "Just for Girls" pages of the Girl Scouts Web site for more information (http://jfg.girlscouts.org).

Join with Your Family

Another option is to join with your family to do community service. This is a great way to help others, while strengthening the bonds within your own family. Many families celebrate holidays—Thanksgiving, for instance—by making and serving food at a soup kitchen, or they welcome spring by planting a community garden together. Try to find an activity that every family member is interested in, and then figure out how you might turn that into doing something for your community. If your family is musically inclined, entertaining at a nursing home or senior citizen center might work.

What if you're a family of writers? One idea is to start a newsletter that you can post in public places (always get permission first), describing volunteer opportunities in your community. How would you divide up the work? One family member could do research about

Liz Says:

My mom and I both like to write and give advice, so when my mom asked me if I wanted to join her in writing an advice column online as part of the Girl Scout Web site, I jumped at the chance. It's hard to believe that we've been doing this for four years. Reviewing the questions that girls ask (on every topic you can imagine, and some you probably can't) and deciding together which ones we're going to answer brings us closer together, even when we don't always agree on the best way to handle a particular issue. It feels so great when people write back after we've answered a question and they tell us that we really helped them. But even when they don't, I still feel good knowing that I'm doing my best to help other people.

agencies that need volunteers, another could make up the kind of sparkling copy that inspires readers to reach out to help, and a third could respond to mail inquiries.

Decisions, Decisions, Decisions

If you've read this far in this chapter, you've probably already thought about what issue you want to deal with and with whom you will work. What other decisions are left for you to make?

Making sure that the people or organization you are interested in helping really want your support is a critical step. You might be thinking: *Why would someone* not *want my assistance?* Sometimes, your age is an issue. That is, some agencies don't want volunteers who are not eighteen or older or at least in high school. You might be able to change their minds. But if the agency is a large one with lots of rules and regulations that are hard to change, you might prefer to spend your time looking for a more welcoming place instead of working hard to get them to accept you. Of course, that's a decision only you can make.

Selecting an Organization

How do you go about finding out whether you've selected an organization that will want you as a volunteer? Ask—by letter, telephone, or e-mail. Just make sure you include enough information so that whoever receives your inquiry will be positively impressed. While it's easier—and certainly tempting—to have a parent make the initial phone call or write the first letter, an organization is bound to be impressed by your sense of responsibility when you're the one who makes the contact. It's not a bad idea, however, to have a parent check over a draft of your letter before you stick it in the mail, or practice a phone conversation with you. See figure 3 for a sample letter.

Figure 3. A Sample Letter

Your Address
Today's Date

Name and Title of Person You're Writing To
Address

Dear [Use the person's name if you can find out who is in charge of volunteers] or To Whom It May Concern:

I am a [your age]-year-old girl interested in doing volunteer work with [name of the organization]. My experience includes [previous volunteer or school positions]. I am available [number] hours a week [or month] and can start on [date]. You may call me at [your telephone number] or e-mail me at [e-mail address]. Or I will contact you within the next two weeks to discuss how I can help your organization meet its goals. [You might want to describe specific goals such as "help children learn to read" or "find homes for homeless animals" or "entertain the residents of a senior citizen center."]

Sincerely,
Your signature
Your typed or printed name

Once you've mailed your letter, wait a while before contacting the organization by telephone. You probably want to show your interest, but you don't want to come across as a pest.

Remember that if you decide to make a phone call, be prepared for any number of possibilities—a machine on the other end, a receptionist who has only been on the job one day and barely knows who she's working for, or a busy executive who doesn't have time to deal with a long introduction from you. In fact, getting to the point quickly is good advice for almost any phone conversation—except, of course, if you're talking to a close friend, and a long, leisurely conversation is the point.

If you have decided to volunteer with a group of other kids, choose one person to be the spokesperson. But before any contact is made with the community agency, work out these important details:

How much time does each one of you have to volunteer?
When are you available?
What experience do you have?
How will you get to and from your volunteer work?

Answering "I don't know" to most questions is not a great start to the world of volunteer work. On the other hand, making a promise that you can't keep is not a good beginning, either. So do your homework ahead of time. If you honestly can't answer a specific question, saying, "I'll have to find out and let you know," is a mature way to respond. Just remember to get back to the person as soon as possible with the requested information.

Getting Permission

Since you're not an adult, you will need to get permission from various people before starting your community service. Making sure your parents approve is the first step, but some other people probably need to give their permission as well. And most of the time, that permission should be in writing so there'll be no confusion later on. Depending on the kind of work you're going to be doing and where you'll be doing it, you may need to get permission from your school principal, your teacher, your Girl Scout leader, or the person in charge at a community organization (perhaps the head librarian or director of volunteers). Sometimes, a standard form is used, but in other situations, you may be expected to show up with a signed and dated permission letter.

Keeping Track of Your Work

More and more schools are requiring students to do community service. If that's a requirement in your school, some kind of form is likely to be used to help you keep track of what you did and how much time you spent on your project. You may just look at this paperwork as a waste of time. But you never know when you might need this information.

Example: Perhaps in a few years, when you're applying for a job or to college, you can point out with confidence that you spent "fifty hours reading stories to preschoolers at a public library over a period of eight months." Doesn't that sound better than saying that you "spent a few weeks, maybe a few months—well, it could have been a year—reading to kids who were in second grade, or perhaps they were in kindergarten, or maybe they were actually preschoolers"?

If you don't have a form, you can create your own or use table 6-1. In the Comments section, you might describe particular successes (for example, "I finally got Jessie to read a full sentence without help") or issues you need help with (for example, "What else can I do to deal with Ali's shyness?").

Besides being an accurate reminder of what, when, and how you did something, a chart can also help you track your accomplishments. "Wow!" you might exclaim when you review your charts: you tutored twenty-three different kids at the library during the course of a year. Making a difference in the lives of twenty-three children—now that's something to be really

Table 6-1. Community Service Project

Name: _____   Grade: _____

Date	Amount of Time	What I Did	Comments

proud of! But remember, it's not all about numbers. If you helped just one person who otherwise would not have gotten that assistance, you've made an important difference.

Setting Goals

Do you ever set goals for your schoolwork or for relationships? Maybe you've said that you're going to spend at least an hour studying each night or that you're going to avoid getting into fights with your younger brother every day. Setting goals for community work is like that. You decide what you're going to shoot for. You might decide that you will sing and play piano at a nursing home once a month for the whole year. That's one kind of goal—you decide the amount of time you'll spend on an activity. Then you track your time to see whether you've reached your goal.

Accomplishing something specific is another type of goal. Maybe you've decided to teach a group of young girls how to kick a soccer ball properly. Your aim might be to get each one to score at least one goal.

Why bother setting goals? They help you to reach for something. They may be just the push you need to continue when you encounter setbacks, like when one little kid just can't seem to kick a ball into the net. If your goal is to make

Liz Says:

I've heard that community service can be helpful when you want to apply for a job or go to college. Guidance counselors and teachers say that you should put volunteer work on your résumé and job or college applications. My brother and his friends who are in high school say that colleges will look more favorably on someone who has done a lot of community service than someone who hasn't. For example, if a college has one more space left and two candidates are equally smart and talented and have received the same good grades, the college would probably choose the person who had done a lot of community service over the one who did very little or none. Even though jobs and college might seem far away, it's a good idea to start community service now. You will have more time to learn what you're good at, how to get things done, and do more of it. It will also look better if you did one kind of community service for a long time than if you only did something for a short period of time, even if you did the same amount of work. Doing one service for a long time shows that you are committed to it.

My fifteen-year-old brother, Rob, tutors kids at the public library every Wednesday afternoon, and the kids have gotten to know him. One of them even gave him a nickname, but it's one he doesn't like, so I can't write it here. Most of his friends also do volunteer work. One tutors at the library with him, and another is a referee for youth soccer games. These are the types of community service that don't seem like work at all.

sure that every child gets one goal, you're more likely to keep at it. Maybe you'll give the girl who keeps kicking the ball away from the goal instead of into it just a bit more practice time. Imagine how good you'll feel when you actually meet your goal. What is your goal for making a difference in your community?

Projects That Make a Difference

Every town has lots of needs and challenges. Below are twenty-five project ideas for making a difference in your community—either on your own or with others. Before you get too far along in the planning process, make sure you obtain the appropriate permissions. For instance, if you want to put up flyers at school, you'll need to get permission first from a school administrator. If you're planning a show for hospital patients, you'll need the okay from a hospital official. And if you're going to plant on public property, make sure you're allowed to do so.

1. Organize a talent show for younger children.

2. Make a flyer with safety tips for riding a bicycle (for example, "Always wear a helmet") and get permission to post it in a shop that sells bikes.

3. Prepare a safety announcement (maybe on wearing car seat belts) that can be given over the public address system at your school.

4. Volunteer to teach other kids how to draw cartoon characters.

5. Plant flowers in a public place, like on an abandoned lot.

6. Weed a garden or mow a lawn for an elderly neighbor.

7. Help a neighbor care for a toddler.

8. Sing or play a musical instrument at a senior citizen center or nursing home.

9. Paint a room or a wall in a community agency.

10. Ask an adult who works in the field of substance abuse prevention to give a talk at your school. Handle the arrangements and give the introduction.

11. Start a "toiletries" drive, collecting small bags of sample soaps, shampoos, and toothpaste to donate to a women's shelter.

12. Collect used books, and donate them to your public or school library or to an after-school program like a branch of the Boys and Girls Clubs.

13. Start a recycling club to help the kids at your school get into the recycling habit.

14. Tutor younger kids in math or reading.

15. Teach someone how to use a word-processing computer software program.

16. Help clean up a neglected park or playground.

17. Make a tape of a story to donate to an organization that works with kids who are blind or have a learning disability.

18. Draw and put up posters at school with antismoking messages.

19. Distribute water to runners or walkers at a race that's raising money to fight a disease, such as breast cancer.

20. Organize a child care program so that parents can attend an evening PTA or PTO meeting.

21. Collect cans of food and other nonperishable food items from friends and neighbors and donate them to a local food pantry serving poor people.

22. Play cards with seniors at a nursing home or senior citizen center.

23. Organize a tag or yard sale where people can donate kitchen gadgets and books, with the profits going to a local charity.

24. Perform a comedy act at the pediatric ward of a hospital.

25. Make holiday cards for holidays that aren't celebrated very often, and distribute those cards at a shelter, senior citizen center, or hospital. Flag Day, anyone?

With your friends and family, add even more ideas to the list.

How Well Did It Work?

Before you start working on a service project, you assume that it's going to be successful. But not every project works. Some fail because there wasn't enough planning. Maybe you and your friend had the brilliant idea to make

My Girl Scout troop gets involved in a lot of community service. We go to nursing homes in December and around Valentine's Day and sing songs related to the holidays. We may be the only group of eleven-, twelve-, and thirteen-year-old girls who know all the words to love songs that were written in the late 1800s and early 1900s! We also prepare and distribute cards, and almost all the people who live at the nursing home are glad to get a handmade card from us. And they're a great audience. Last year, in the middle of my solo dance piece, I forgot a part of it. So I made something up and just kept dancing in time to the music. No one seemed to notice—except, of course, for the girl in my troop who was in my dance class. The applause at the end sounded great.

Right now, most of the girls in my troop are working on our Girl Scout Silver Award project. You have to do thirty hours of community service on one project along with fulfilling a bunch of other requirements. Our project is teaching a troop of Daisy Girl Scouts sport skills. The Daisies are only five or six years old, and they're so cute. Besides, it's fun to have younger girls looking up to us—we're role models for them. We teach them skills like throwing and catching, and kicking and hitting balls, and how to move quickly and accurately. They're so proud of themselves when they do well, and we encourage them to keep working at getting better. The girls really enjoy learning and having fun with us, and we get just as much out of the experience as they do, maybe even more. One little girl who was really shy came out of her shell when I played one-on-one with her. Her leader said it was the first time this girl had fully participated in a group activity. Can you imagine what a great feeling that gave me?

crafts to raise money for an animal shelter in your town. Great idea, but unless you plan to buy or have donated all the items you need to make the crafts, decide on a date well in advance, get all the permissions you need, and publicize the craft sale and the cause being supported, you'll be left with a great idea and not much else to show for it.

Sometimes projects do not succeed because they were too ambitious. That means that maybe you bit off more than you could chew within the time frame available. Maybe you decided in early December to organize a puppet show for hospitalized kids during the Christmas, Hanukkah, Ramadan, and Kwanzaa season. Starting at that late date doesn't allow you the time you need to get your supplies, obtain permissions from hospital staff, and find others who will work with you.

There may also be times when you think you've done everything right, but you still didn't achieve your goals. What then? Just walk away from the project feeling frustrated and disappointed, maybe even angry, and forget all about it? Not if you want to learn from your mistakes and do a better job next time. And even if you didn't accomplish what you set out to do, that doesn't automatically mean that the project was a total failure. Evaluate what worked and what didn't. Have you ever heard the saying "When life hands you a lemon, make lemonade"? In other words, you could look at your experience as one big sour lemon that left a bitter taste in your mouth. Or you could use the incident in a positive way to develop a skill—you made lemonade with a lemon in your life. Perhaps you learned how to plan your time better—that's a big glass of lemonade. Or maybe, you realized that you couldn't do everything yourself.

On page 150, you'll find a tool that will help you better understand what worked well and what you might want to change when you do a community project like this in the future. Use it exactly as you see it here, or change it for the particular circumstances of your project.

In addition to judging the success of a project yourself, you can obtain important information by asking the people you are working with some questions about their experience. On page 151, you'll find an example of that

How Did This Project Work?

1. What part of the project was most successful?

_____

_____

_____

2. What didn't work as well as you had expected? Why not?

_____

_____

_____

3. What would you do differently the next time you do something like this? Why?

_____

_____

_____

4. What was the most important thing you learned from doing this project?

_____

_____

_____

kind of tool. Of course, you would have to fill in the blanks to describe your project. For instance, if you read stories at the library, question 1 would read "What did you like most about story time at the library?" These specific questions might not apply to some projects; for those you'd have to develop your own set of questions. In other cases, you might not be able to ask questions at all of the people you are doing something for. It would be kind of tough to ask babies whether they liked the toys they received. (Well, you could ask, but they wouldn't be able to answer with words.) But you could get a sense of what they thought by observing the expressions on their faces. So do whatever will work to learn how well a project worked.

What Do You Think?

1. What did you like most about _____?

   _____

   _____

   _____

2. What did you like least about _____?

   _____

   _____

   _____

3. How would you change _____ to make it better?

   _____

   _____

   _____

4. Would you like to _____ again? Why or why not?

_____

_____

_____

What Do You Get Out of All This Work?

Do you remember reading earlier in this chapter that one of the reasons to get involved is because this experience will help you grow? How does that happen?

For starters, the kinds of activities you will be doing when you serve your community will help you learn new skills. If you're working in a garden, you're learning about different kinds of plants, why worms are good for the soil (they really are), when certain kinds of plants should go into the ground, and how plants should be cared for. What if your project is preparing a script for an announcement about a food drive at school? You're learning about the best way to reach people, how writing words for a speech is different from writing something that will be read silently, and how to obtain information about the number of people in your community who are hungry because they don't have enough money for food.

As you're learning new skills, you might uncover some talents you never knew you had. Some shy kids have learned that they really enjoy public speaking after they made presentations about an issue close to their hearts.

Example: A girl who speaks at the town council meeting about why a traffic light is needed at a busy intersection, might be surprised and pleased at the way she is able to quiet the room with her account of how two people had been killed there within the past year. Shy people might learn they have power when they speak, and kids who've never handled tools might learn that they have a knack for putting things together. Who knows what you'll discover about yourself through doing something for others? Maybe you'll awaken an interest in an area that will become a career sometime in the future. You might find that you want to become a politician after you see the impact your words have on an audience or that you want to learn much more about the environment so you can make a really big difference someday.

⊚ ⊚ ⊚

Doing service is a great way to meet people, ones whose paths you might never have crossed. And because you're all working on the same project, you start off having at least two things in common: the desire to help others and an interest in a particular cause (children with disabilities, literacy, or hunger, for example). So friendship might be a side benefit of helping your

Community Service to Careers: Make a Connection

- Reducing water pollution— marine biologist, water quality scientist, or chemical engineer
- Speaking out about an issue—lawyer, politician, or TV news anchor
- Racing to raise money— athlete, coach, or salesperson
- Entertaining at a nursing home—actress, singer, or musician
- Organizing a tag or yard sale—store manager, marketing expert, or business owner
- Making flyers about safety—physician, designer, or writer of advertisements
- Reading to kids—publisher, librarian, or teacher
- Training people to use computers—software developer, professor, or Web site designer
- Organizing sports events— recreational therapist, events manager, or agent

community. And a friend who cares enough about others to get up and help out is someone you probably want around.

Have you ever heard anyone say, "I get more out of giving than the people I give to"? People say that because it feels good to help others, to do something unselfishly, to make a difference in someone's life. In chapter 1, you read about how people see themselves. Which of these two statements would you rather say about yourself: "I'm the kind of person who helps others" or "I'm the kind of person who thinks first and always about my own needs"? Which would make you feel proud of who you are? Not hard to answer, is it? Most people would like to be able to say that the first statement reflects how they feel about themselves. So, if you do reach out to help others in need, you're doing something for yourself, too—taking a big step toward feeling good about who you are.

So much good can come from doing good that it's hard to imagine why some people don't want to get involved. For some kids, it's hard to get out of the rut of their everyday routine—school, homework, eating, TV, talking on the telephone, shopping, sending e-mail messages to friends, sleeping. If you've already started taking action to serve your community, keep it up. And if you're getting ready to make a commitment to action, congratulations! If you're still undecided, think for a moment about what your town or city would be like if everyone just took care of their own needs and didn't reach out to others. Not a pretty picture. So get out there in your community and make a difference. After all, it's where you live.

CHAPTER 7

Global Citizens

Embracing Diversity and Making Friends Around the World

Best friends Brianna and Ayako look as different as any two twelve-year-olds could. One is tall; the other, short. One is African American; the other, Asian American. But what they have in common are the important things—from their interest in reading historical novels to what they value in a friendship: loyalty, sharing, and a sense of humor. While some people might notice and care about the differences between the girls, Brianna and Ayako know that they couldn't be closer, even if they were sisters.

If this planet were filled with all fair people, everyone would understand that the differences among people enrich the world. How boring it would be if everyone followed the same customs and traditions, ate the same kinds of food, celebrated the same holidays, built the same houses, and played the same games. Fortunately, people all over the globe are different in lots of ways. Unfortunately, the world is not as ideal as it could be. While some people appreciate the beauty of the earth's diversity, others do not.

This chapter explores the importance of being a global citizen—recognizing your place in the world and appreciating the value of other people and their cultures. You'll also have an opportunity to "think globally and act locally." That is, you don't have to travel to another land to attack a global issue, like the destruction of forests in Africa and South America. What you do right here at home can make an enormous impact on the world, even help to save disappearing rain forests. Wouldn't you like to play your part in combating global issues like hunger and illiteracy or eliminating the prejudice and discrimination that ignorant people sometimes display?

Some Global
Issues

Hunger
Poverty
Unvaccinated
    children
Overuse of the
    land
Child abuse
    and neglect
War
Illiteracy
Water pollution
Not enough
    water for
    drinking or
    farming
Diseases such
    as AIDS
Overpopulation
    and crowding
Inflation
Disappearing
    rain forests
Air pollution
Unemployment
Few opportuni-
    ties for
    schooling for
    girls
Homelessness
Child labor
Endangered
    plant and
    animal
    species

Explore Your Heritage

Before you can truly value other people's backgrounds, it helps to learn about and appreciate your own heritage. That doesn't just mean finding out that your great-great-uncle Joe lived in Wyoming in the late 1800s or that your great-grandmother traveled by ship to the United States, speaking not a word of English. Understanding your heritage means learning the stories of your ancestors, learning how they arrived in this country and why they came, how they grew and prepared their food, what jobs they held, what hardships they endured, what rituals and customs they brought with them, how they practiced their religion, what they wore, what kind of lifestyle they followed, and what language they spoke.

How do you find all this out?

Do This:

Start by asking your parents whether they have old family scrapbooks and photo albums you can look at. Who knows what you'll discover up in an attic trunk or hidden away on the top shelf of a closet, aside from cobwebs and dead bugs. Lots of families have saved old photos of people they can no longer identify. You might

Liz Says:

When my grandmother died, we found a big carton of pictures she had kept at her house. Because we didn't have time to sort through the box at that time, we just stored it in the attic and forgot about it. Not too long ago, I was looking for a blanket in the attic when I came across that box. I took it downstairs and started looking through the contents. I found all sorts of interesting pictures. Some of the small snapshots my mom and I put into albums, but most of the pictures went into envelopes to sort some other time. We found about ten copies of a picture of my great-great-grandfather.

We also discovered two pictures that particularly intrigued us. One was of a 1932 graduation picture of boys from a junior high school. The year was too late to be my grandfather's class picture. I really wanted to identify the person in the picture who was related to me, but why this picture was kept remains a mystery. The other picture that attracted my attention was on tin or some other metal, and it was signed. Perhaps the woman was an actress and that was the way autographed photos were sent long ago. All I know is that we have a signed metal photo of Becky Schnapps, whoever she might be.

need to ask other relatives whether they can recognize the old woman wearing a shawl or the little baby holding a rattle. In your journal or on the previous page, write about your most interesting discoveries:

Create Oral Histories

What else can you do? Talk to the oldest members of your family you can find. If they don't live close by, telephone calls work, too. But check with your parents first. A relative who has a lot to say can really run up a phone bill! Create an oral history of each person's life. How? Start with a list of questions, not those that can be answered with simple yes and no responses. Something like, "Were you happy as a child?" would not be a good question, but "What is your happiest memory as a child?" is much better. See the difference? Some other effective questions are "What kinds of games did you play with your friends when you were my age?" and "What household chores did you have to do, and how much time did they take?" After you hear the answer to that last question, you might never complain again about having to fold your clothes when they come out of the dryer. That's a whole lot easier than using a scrub board to wash your clothes, one at a time, and then hanging them out on a clothesline to dry!

Now that you have some idea of how to obtain solid information, prepare your questions on the Oral History Form in figure 4, find some relatives, and start interviewing. If you have permission to do so, use a tape recorder or video camera to keep and share oral histories. If you or your relatives want to exchange letters or e-mail messages, those are other ways of collecting old family stories. Do whatever feels comfortable for you and your older relative. Once you're all done, you might be amazed to find out how fascinating your ancestors really were.

Share what you've learned with your friends, particularly with those who come from a different religious or ethnic background. And ask them to let you have a peek into their religious and cultural practices. You may be interested in finding out how different groups use candles in holiday celebrations or learning the hymns or songs that mark special occasions.

Figure 4. Oral History Form

Oral History of _____

Born in 19_____ in the town/city of _____.

Questions

1.

_____

_____

2.

_____

_____

3.

_____

_____

Speaking Another Language

If someone in your family speaks a language other than English, you might take advantage of that and start picking up some phrases. Since the world is becoming increasingly connected, knowing a language in addition to English

Liz Says:

In fifth grade I had to make a family tree for a school project and something else that had to do with my heritage. I made a book with a bunch of family stories and pictures. By doing this project, I learned a lot about my family. My mom told me about some of her father's experiences as a soldier during World War II. And she told me about the skits she and her cousins used to perform for their parents. My grandma—my father's mother—often tells me stories about when my dad was little or about what life was like when she was young. The stories are sometimes quite funny, and they're always interesting to me since they're part of my heritage.

One story my grandmother told me goes like this: When she was little, she, along with her brother and cousin, sometimes visited their grandparents' farm. The children often played in the barn, but they were not allowed to go up to the loft where the hay was kept. Sometimes, they would go up on top anyway and make tunnels through the hay. They loved talking and playing games up in the loft, but the three of them promised never to tell anyone. One day, they were playing in the tunnels when their grandfather came in to get some hay. My grandmother was so surprised when she heard him come in that she jumped up and fell out of the loft and almost landed on a pitchfork that was next to the ladder!

is very useful. And if you are fluent in another language because you were born in another country or because some members of your family use that tongue frequently, try to stay in practice. You never know when that language will help you land a job, get into a special school program, enjoy a trip to another country (people in other places really appreciate it when you make the effort to use their language when you're visiting), or maybe even help you meet a cute boy. But if you don't use the language frequently, it will not be available for you at the precise moment when you need it most.

If you are fluent in a foreign language, don't assume that no one else knows what you're saying. Imagine how embarrassed you'd be if you used your Chinese to say something a little less than positive about a woman at the mall, only to find out from her angry expression that she knew exactly what you were saying!

If You Were Adopted

If you were adopted, you may know a lot about the heritage of your mom and dad who love you and live with you. And you may know all about your birth parents, too. But maybe you don't. You may have questions about the heritage of your birth parents, or you may not. You may be

Liz Says:

My grandparents speak several different languages, since they have lived in many different parts of the world. Hungarian was their first language. I don't speak it fluently, but I know some words and a few little phrases, such as "Come here" and "I love you." Maybe they're not the most useful words, but it's a lot of fun learning. Eventually I hope I'll be able to understand more of what my grandparents are saying when they speak in Hungarian. Right now I'm studying Spanish in school and I realize that becoming fluent in that language will be very valuable, wherever I live and whatever jobs I will have in the future.

interested in finding out more, or you may not be curious at all—at least not right now. However you feel is okay.

If you are curious, it may be hard for your parents to understand or accept your need to know more. They may feel that you will somehow love them less if you learn more about the background of your birth parents. Reassure them that your love for them will not lessen but that you will feel more comfortable about yourself if you have a fuller picture of where and who you came from. And if you don't really need or want to discover more, that's okay, too—you already have a family heritage to be proud of.

What Can You Learn About People from Around the World?

As part of your schoolwork, you may have learned about people who live in different countries around the world. Perhaps you've even had to do a project about a particular place. Sometimes, just because you have a school assignment on a topic, the learning feels like a burden, something you just have to get through. But the fact is, finding out about distant lands and discovering how people live in those faraway places can be fascinating. Here's a project for you, but don't think of it as a task you are required to complete. Instead, imagine that you're traveling to a far-off country, all expenses paid. Who knows—you might get so excited about what you find out that you'll want to start saving up right away so you can actually visit one day.

Decide Where to "Go"

How should you decide where to go on your imaginary trip? Here are several ways to choose:

♣ Ask a friend to give you a letter of the alphabet, but don't tell her what you're going to do with it. You then find a country that starts with that letter.

✤ While your eyes are closed, twirl a globe. With your outstretched arm, point to a place. Pointing to the couch or the window gets you another turn. If your finger landed on a body of water, you can try again or investigate that ocean, river, or lake.

✤ If you have an atlas, ask a family member to give you a number from 1 to whatever number of pages are in the book. Turn to that page, and you've got a country, maybe several of them. Pick one.

✤ If a friend or classmate was born in another country, perhaps you'd like to consider choosing it as your place.

✤ If you were born in another country but came here when you were too young to remember much, you might want to find out more about that place.

✤ What's the first letter of your first or last name? Search out a country that also begins with that letter.

✤ Think about the last movie you saw that took place in a different country. Okay, that's your place!

Don't get all caught up trying to figure out which decision-making method you should use to make your choice. Just pick one and start exploring. In fact, if there's a place you were curious about even before you started reading this chapter, don't even bother with picking and choosing—you already know where you want to go in your dreams.

Discover a New Place and New People

Finding out about the life of a girl your age in the country you've chosen is an interesting way to start your investigation. What questions do you have? What would you ask her if you actually met her? Does she go to school? (Believe it or not, in some countries, girls do not attend school. But before you start packing your bags, you might want to learn some more facts about those places.) What do her parents do? What does her family do for entertainment?

How does she dress? Does she have a job? (Yes, lots of girls in countries out-side the United States work to support their families.) Does she expect to have a career when she grows up? What types of games does she play? What is her home like? Who does she share it with? Are boys and girls treated dif-ferently? In what ways?

You can add lots more questions to these. But how do you find answers? The library is a good place to start. You can ask a reference librarian or check the library computer to help you find books about the country you've chosen. Nonfiction books are not the only way to go. You might learn the most by reading stories that take place in "your" country. Most authors who create sto-ries about kids who live in other countries have done lots of research before they begin to write. So pick out a book with your country as the story's back-drop, and expand your world.

You can also use the Internet. Not only will you find a tremendous num-ber of details about almost any place you're interested in, you'll also get to "see" your country in glorious color.

Many girls your age around the world cannot go to school. Some must work to help their families purchase food, clothing, medi-cine, or shelter. Other girls are needed to care for younger sib-lings or do household chores. Still others cannot afford the cost of getting an education. Sadly, some girls are not permitted to go to school at all—in some places, only boys are allowed to be in school.

A travel agent is another source of information. You don't have to pretend that you're twenty-three and actually taking a trip. Most agents will be happy to help you—after all, you might recommend them to your parents or become a paying client yourself in the future.

Moving to a New Country

Lots of families move every year. Some move just down the street, while others move halfway across the world. If your family is moving to a different country, whether for six months or maybe years, what can you do to prepare yourself? You can use one or more of the methods described on the previous pages to find out about the place you're going to.

Don't ignore your feelings—both the positive and negative ones—that will probably sprout up. Maybe you're worried about whether you'll be able to make new friends or devastated that you'll be leaving your very best friend just when your life is getting really exciting. Perhaps you're concerned that you'll have trouble learning the language that's spoken in the country you're going to live in. But you might also be excited about meeting new people and discovering new places—perhaps a famous historic site you've only seen in books. In the space on page 167, describe your doubts as well as your hopes and dreams about your future home. And don't forget to talk to your parent or another understanding adult who can help you cope with the ups and downs of your feelings.

Maybe it's not your family who's moving far away but your close friend and her family. That's tough, too. Before the two of you separate, make a pact to stay in touch. And these days, it's easier than ever before—e-mail can help friends share the latest news even when they're thousands of miles away from each other. Old-fashioned letter writing still works, and you can exchange little gifts—stamps, magazine articles, posters, and photos—from time to time to show that you still hold an important place in each other's lives. But remember to be open to new friendships, too, and recognize that your friend will need to move on in her new life as well. That doesn't mean you care about each other any less. It's just that kids your age need to have friends to do things with, and that's kind of tough with someone who lives a continent away. And think about this plus—you'll have an international pen pal you already feel committed to.

Think Globally, Act Locally

"I'm just one person," you may be thinking. "What can I do to change the world?" Maybe more than you think! Imagine a girl with an idea for

addressing a global issue. She tells herself, "Who would listen to me? I'm just twelve years old." So her brainstorm stays in her brain, while the world problem grows. What if, instead of keeping her idea to herself, she is determined to use it to make a difference?

Liz Says:

When I was six years old, one of my best friends had to move to Charlotte, North Carolina, because of her father's business. A few years later she moved again—this time to Japan, where her parents were born and her grandparents lived. We wrote letters back and forth every so often, but not very much. Usually, we only wrote to each other when it was one of our birthdays or during the holiday season. Even though we really wanted to keep our friendship going, writing letters was hard. One time, after I hadn't written for several months, I wrote a letter to her, and the letter came back with something stamped on it in Japanese. I compared that address to the one that was the return address on the last letter that she had sent me. The address was the same, so I assumed that she had moved and that the Japanese phrase stamped on the envelope said something like "not at this address." I waited for her to send me a letter so I could write to her again. I never got a letter.

Finally, my dad had the smart idea of finding her new address through her dad's company. He went to the company's Web site and wrote a letter saying who we were and who we were trying to locate. Sure enough, my dad's detective work paid off. We received a wonderful e-mail message from her father, which included their new address. This time I'm really going to keep in touch with her and write to her more often. I hope that one day I'll actually get to see my friend in person again.

Have you thought about what you can get involved in? Start by looking at the list of issues on page 156. Then look back at the steps in chapter 6 for taking action in your local community—except this time you're going to figure out what you need to do about an issue in the *global* community. Here are some suggestions for you and your friends and family:

* Educate people about the issue you picked—make posters, write a letter to the school or local newspaper, or organize a panel discussion for a school assembly program. Be sure you get your facts right before you make them public.

* Donate part of your allowance or extra money you earn for doing special chores or birthday money to an organization that is doing something about your issue. Ask a parent or teacher to help you find a reputable group that will use your money for the cause rather than for administrative costs.

* Adopt a heifer, a whale, or an acre of a rain forest—that doesn't mean you're bringing the animal or trees into your home, but you're contributing money to keep them safe and healthy.

* Organize a boycott of a product that is made using child labor or unfair labor practices. Before you take action, make sure you have your facts straight. It's not fair to hurt a company based on rumors that turn out to be untrue, something that has been known to happen.

* Enter or help out at a race or other event that has been set up to raise money for an international cause. You might get people to pledge a certain amount for each mile you walk, or you might give out water at stations as racers running for a cause come by.

* Do something in your community that has global effects. For instance, help your family conserve gas by convincing them to walk rather than hop into a car for a short trip—the extra exercise you all get is not a bad thing, either. Or you might make a commitment to help neighbors recycle paper to reduce the number of trees that need to be cut down.

Gather some other ideas from friends and families to add to this list. But more important than the length of this list is your determination to learn as much as you can about the issue, make a plan, get other people to work with you, and accomplish something.

Liz Says:

As a community service project, my Girl Scout troop bought or made New Year's gifts for children who lived in an orphanage in China. We wrapped the gifts in red paper, which represents good luck, and sent them out. A few weeks later, we received a small envelope from the orphanage with pictures of the children, mostly girls, opening their gifts along with individual letters from some of the kids. One boy wrote to me, telling me a little about himself. His letter was in Chinese, but a friend's friend translated it for me, so I found out that he liked to play basketball and chess.

Being Different, Being the Same

Think about all the kids in your class or in your neighborhood. How many different ways can you divide them? Here's an obvious one—kids are either girls or boys. Maybe they're members of a whole bunch of different religions and races. Some are tall, while others are short. Perhaps some classmates are thin; others are heavier. How important are these differences to you? Do you choose your friends by how similar they are to you? What are the similarities that really count in a relationship? Why did you become close to your best friend? Not because she was the same size as you, was it? That's not a very good basis for a friendship. But some people only trust those people who are similar to themselves in the way they worship or in the color of their skin. They might not invite someone to a party if she was born in a different country or has a disability. You wouldn't call their attitudes or their actions very fair, would you?

What Is Sexism?

Has your mom or your grandma ever told you about a time when someone wouldn't let her do something or required that she act in a certain way for one reason only—because she was female? Lots of women can recall specific situations like that from their preteen and teen years.

Example: Perhaps they were discouraged from joining the math club at school when they were in junior high or made fun of because they were interested in doing science experiments. Maybe they were prevented from joining a sports team or made to do chores while their brothers played—just because they were girls or young women.

ⓖ ⓖ ⓖ

When those kinds of things happen, sexism is at work. It's a kind of prejudiced attitude. While sexism is not as likely to turn itself into outright discrimination today, that doesn't mean you will not face prejudice against females in some form at some time in your life. And when the signs are subtle and indirect, you may not see them as wrong. In fact, when sexism is really subtle, you may not even notice. But whether it's a firm "No, you can't do that!" or an ambiguous "Are you sure you really want to do that?" you are losing an opportunity to grow and learn. And that just isn't fair—whatever you call it.

Start becoming more aware of how you might be held back by sexism. Look around at a toy store, for instance. Some are still organized by "boy" and "girl" sections. What do you find in the boy sections? Some of the games and toys, like trucks and action figures, lots of girls would like to play with—and do—so why are they in a section called "Boys"? And what's in the section labeled "Girls"? Mostly pink—not that there's anything wrong with that color, but it can get a bit nauseating when it's thrown at you all the time. And dolls—lots of them in every color, size, and type. Again, there's nothing wrong with dolls. But why deprive boys of a chance to imagine and learn to take care of a baby, too?

Where else might you see sexism at work? Unfortunately sometimes in school. Girls, particularly quiet ones who need a moment to collect their thoughts before responding to a teacher's questions, are occasionally ignored by teachers who pay attention to aggressive boys yelling out the answers. In some schools and families, girls are expected to not like math and, even worse, not be good at it. Again, that's sexism doing its damage.

The words you see in books and hear on TV and in conversation influence how you think about the world. What happens when you hear language that is sexist? If a firefighter is referred to as a *fireman,* do you ever picture a woman in your mind? Very unlikely. Same goes for *policeman* versus *police officer.* What about *mankind* or *man* when *people* is meant? Get the point? Get into the habit of using language that isn't sexist, and help others do the same. Check out your school newspaper or any magazines you read, and see whether the language being used is really fair to all its readers. And if it's not, you know what to do.

Sexist Language	A Better Way to Say It
fireman	firefighter
policeman	police officer
mankind	people
salesman	salesperson
chairman	chairperson

Why Are People Prejudiced?

When Yolanda's classmates mock her accent, or Samantha gets teased about being the shortest kid in her grade, or Katie's peers laugh because her clothes have obviously been worn by several others before her and they don't exactly fit, these girls are the targets of prejudiced minds. The wounds may not be bloody, but they hurt just the same. Why is it that some kids are sensitive to the feelings of others, while others don't have a clue about someone else's viewpoint? For starters, some kids learn to be understanding from parents or other family members who are role models of kindness and fairness.

Example: A mom, stopped in her car at a red light, patiently waits as the elderly man with a walker moves slowly across the street even though she's late for an appointment and the light has now been green for ten seconds. A dad, as class parent on a trip, chooses to sit on the bus next to the kid no one wants to be with—and tries to make him feel comfortable. A grandmother gently, but firmly, corrects a young grandchild who uses a not-so-nice term to describe a neighbor of another race. An uncle finds time in his busy life to volunteer at a homeless shelter once a month.

6 6 6

What are all these relatives teaching? Vital lessons in tolerance and acceptance.

But what about those people who teach the opposite? Who think that their religion or race is best? Who practice intolerance on a daily basis? Who use hateful language to talk about people who are different from themselves? If some members of your family are less than open to people who are unlike them in any way, are you doomed to be prejudiced? Absolutely not. When your eyes are open to what's fair, your heart and mind will open, too. But it does take thought and practice. And once you start believing in treating people in a just way, it will be hard for you to look the other way when you see injustice or hear prejudiced remarks. Are you ready to teach a family member or two some lessons in acceptance?

What else feeds into prejudice? If you've had very limited face-to-face experience with people who are different from you, it may be hard to be open-minded. Maybe almost all of the people in your community come from similar backgrounds. What can you do? Make an effort to read or watch TV shows about people from different places and with different experiences. As you get older, search out opportunities to interact directly with different kinds of people, instead of relying on spending time only with people you already feel comfortable with because they're so much like you. Lots of great friendships have developed when people reach out to those who are different from them. The media—TV, movies, CDs, magazines, video games—sometimes foster prejudice. How? By depicting people in stereotyped ways. Maybe you're so busy snapping your fingers or tapping your feet to the latest song that you don't detect the negative messages. Strangely enough, you might even have memorized the words without having allowed the meaning to really sink in.

Do This:

Listen—really listen—to the words in the songs played on your favorite radio station. Notice any stereotyping of girls or women? Any nasty language about people of different races? How many positive messages did you hear? You can do the same thing with TV shows—focus on whether the characters treat others with respect and whether they depict characters from a broad range of ethnic and racial groups. When you start paying attention to media messages, you may be unpleasantly surprised by how much stereotyping exists. What can you do? Become a more sensitive media consumer and let others in on what you've learned. You might express your opinion by writing to a newspaper editor or a television station or a TV sponsor. Since most people don't bother to write, your words could carry a lot of weight, speaking for thousands.

Emphasize Abilities

Do you have a disability or do you know someone with one? Millions of people in this country have some kind of disability. Some are more obvious than others. If a girl uses a wheelchair to get around, it would be hard not to notice. But if she has a learning disability, that's harder to see.

Example: Sarah likes the challenge of math puzzles, has a wild sense of humor, and is a terrific caring friend. She also has a visual impairment. Kristen loves to play the flute, choreographs dance moves for herself and her friends, and enjoys exploring new places with her family. She happens to be mentally retarded as well.

⑥ ⑥ ⑥

What's the point of these descriptions? To emphasize the fact that girls with disabilities are always more than their disabilities—they *can* do so much more than they can't.

If you have a disability or care deeply about someone who does, you have probably encountered narrow-minded people who stare or ridicule or avoid. Why do they act that way? Most likely because they're ignorant. Or maybe they never learned from their families to focus on people's abilities, rather than their disabilities. What can you do? Here are a few ideas:

* Get together with like-minded classmates, and see whether you can get permission to hold a "Disabilities Awareness Day (or Week)" at school, in your house of worship, or through Girl Scouting or another youth group—complete with posters, speakers, and refreshments (always a way to draw a crowd).
* Contact an organization to do a workshop (some do this with puppets) that helps kids understand what it's like to have a disability. Perhaps a

teacher, guidance counselor at school, or a librarian can help you locate a group that can put on a workshop like that at a school assembly program.

✽ Start a "Raising Awareness Club" (that doesn't have to be the name) at school. Put on skits or seek out volunteer opportunities in your community. Help promote your club to attract kids you don't know. You might even make some new friends through a club like this—kids who feel strongly about some of the same issues you do.

✽ Write a short story for your school literary magazine that has a character with a disability as a main character. Make sure you provide this kid with a full, interesting life.

✽ Protest—by letter, e-mail, or phone call—instances of disability stereotyping you see on TV shows or commercials or in magazines. Ask friends and relatives to do the same. There's power in numbers.

✽ Don't let ignorant comments slip by unnoticed in conversation or jokes. If someone uses a terrible term like *retard,* don't let that person get away with it. Many kids use that word and other hurtful words without realizing the impact of their choice of biased language. Let them know. It's not easy to confront people when they say something that shows their prejudices. It's even hard to do this with close friends. But think of how proud of yourself you'll be when you stand up to do the right thing. And maybe whoever used the offensive language will think twice before using such words in the future.

✽ Check out your school building and other public places that you use to determine how accessible they are for people with physical disabilities. If you notice areas that are not accessible, bring those to the attention of administrators who can do something about it. Offer to work with them to change things, maybe even helping to raise money to make necessary building alterations.

ⓖ ⓖ ⓖ

The technology that is present today and will become available in the future brings problems from around the world right into your home. You watch vivid news coverage of violent earthquakes a continent away, and you see stories about the spread of a disease unfolding before your eyes as you search the Internet for a homework project. As you grow up, you will find more and more ways to meet these global challenges. But you definitely don't have to wait to get older before you start to take action to make the world a better place. Whether you're correcting a classmate's choice of words to describe someone with a disability or raising money to help the victims of a destructive hurricane or planting trees to replace those lost in a fire, you're making a real difference in the world.

CHAPTER 8

Dream On

Creating—and Managing—Your Future

Close your eyes, and imagine your life five years into the future. What do you see? In the space below and on the next page, describe how you look, what school you're going to, who your friends are, how you spend your free time (hopefully you have some), where you live, and what music you like listening to.

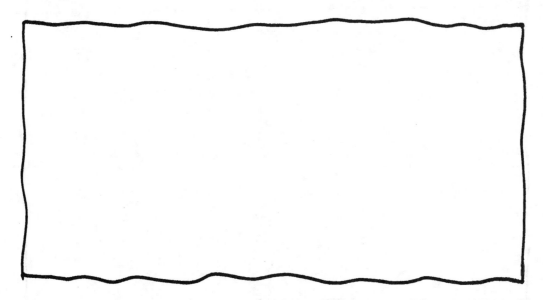

Now, close your eyes again, and this time it's ten years from now. What is your life like? How different is it from what you do at the present time? What do you have to do now to prepare yourself for the kind of life you'd like to have in years to come? That's what this chapter is all about. Dreaming is great, but turning your dreams into reality requires putting your talents to work and going after what you really want without allowing obstacles to stand in the way of success. A little bit of luck might help, too. But don't rely on good fortune finding its way to you. You have to create opportunities and take advantage of those that do appear. Read on and you'll learn some important tips for becoming all you can be.

What's Ahead ?

When you imagined your life in five years, you probably saw yourself as a high school student. Most likely, you already know that your grades and test scores in high school along with the kind of extracurricular and community activities you get involved in will be looked at closely by college admissions staff. Does that mean you can just slack off now and then pull yourself together in the ninth grade when everything begins to count? Well, you could do that, but it's not a wise move. You're at an age when you're developing the kind of study habits and interests that will take you through the high school years. If you let things slide now, you may not be able to pick up the pieces in time to assure yourself of a successful student life in a few years. No, you don't have to spend five hours a night on homework, just to get yourself ready for the future. But it's not a bad idea to learn now how to study or write term papers effectively. Better to get suggestions from parents and teachers now than when the pressure is really on you in a few years.

But don't start worrying now. Instead, start getting accustomed now to the habits that will prepare you for the increased workload and more complicated assignments in high school. If you need to, review the information about school and learning in chapter 5.

Preparing for the High School Years

What are some specific actions you can take now to prepare yourself for the high school years? Here are a few ideas:

* *If you're not already doing so, start reading more than just the books that get assigned in class*. Get recommendations from friends or a librarian. Maybe one of your teachers or a relative can suggest a book she just loved at your age. Just because a novel was published two decades or more ago or took place in another country doesn't mean you won't be able to relate to the characters. For example, family conflict or overcoming adversity are timeless themes. What good will this extra reading do for you? For one, you'll expand your vocabulary, particularly if you take time to notice unfamiliar words and figure out from their context what they mean or look up those words in a dictionary. No, you don't have to stop reading and check out each strange word you come across, but you might jot down each one on a piece of paper and then look them up after you've finished your reading for that day. Besides increasing your vocabulary, reading allows you to explore topics and people you would not ordinarily meet.

* *Pay attention to the news on a regular basis*. That doesn't mean you have to read the daily newspaper from cover to cover every day—although you could if that interested you. But learn what's going on in the world from radio, television news reports, weekly magazines that focus on current events, or the Internet.

* *Start a journal or make writing a part of your everyday life*. The more you write, the better your writing becomes. One of the biggest complaints employers have about their employees is the lack of decent writing skills. Start now to make writing a habit. What can you write about? Anything that interests you. Make up stories for younger siblings or cousins. Describe a favorite food, person, holiday, game, TV show,

movie, CD, book, whatever. Write a letter to the editor of your local newspaper—it doesn't matter whether it gets published. Send a note to a relative you haven't seen for a while or a friend who's moved away and share your latest news. Maybe you think that your writing will only get better if a teacher provides you with a formal critique. Sure that would help—if the teacher is a good writer. But even without an official review of your work, your writing will improve if you keep at it.

❀ *Develop your computer skills.* We don't mean just how to use your computer as a word processor but also how to do research on the Internet, create and send attachments, and how to use a variety of software programs. Take advantage of any computer training your school offers. (Read more about the importance of computers on page 194.)

❀ *Participate in extracurricular activities that can be continued throughout high school.* Being a member of the school band, chorus, or orchestra or playing on a sports team will help you fit in, particularly if you will be attending a high school with a very large student body.

❀ *Increase your creativity.* You may be the smartest kid in your school, but if you aren't a creative thinker, you're not going to go to very interesting places in life. Why? Because creativity is the quality that allows people to invent, to see possibilities that fly right by less creative types. If you were stuck in the rubble of a building crushed by a powerful earthquake, creativity would allow you to come up with several different strategies for getting out, provided you were conscious. Not that the scenario is a likely one for your high school years, but it probably grabbed your attention more than an example related to choosing a unique science research project would have! However, that, too, would benefit from creativity. The point is you'll find lots of opportunities in and out of school to use your creativity. How do you develop that skill? By looking at ordinary situations or objects in new ways—brainstorm a hundred uses for a paper clip or a shoebox. Go ahead. Try that right now. Not only will you be enhancing your creativity, but at least a

Advice from Some High School Students

Rob, fifteen: "High school will probably not be what you expected, but that doesn't mean it won't be good. You'll meet a lot of new people—just try to get along with everyone."

Annie, fourteen: "Don't always try to fit in. Be yourself, and you'll find others who agree with your way of doing things."

Max, sixteen: "From day one, get on good terms with your teachers, and try to stay there."

Jamie, fifteen: "Get involved in community service projects. Not only will they look good on your college applications, but they'll also make you feel good about yourself. And you never know who you'll meet."

Jessie, fifteen: "Relax. Be yourself. High school can be the most stressful experience, but don't let it get to you. With every step you take, remember yourself and just how special you are."

Lauren, sixteen: "At first, high school seems so big, but as you get to know your way around, you'll realize it's really not."

Eliot, sixteen: "High school may seem overwhelming at first, but it's really not if you keep things in perspective."

Stephanie, fourteen: "Join clubs to expand your circle of friends. Otherwise, you'll be stuck just hanging out with all the same kids you knew from middle school."

Samantha, fifteen: "Don't believe that everyone's doing 'it,' whatever 'it' is. They're not."

dozen of your possibilities are likely to be hilarious. Think of a shoebox as a protective head covering or a paper clip as a fingernail cleaner. Just as is the case with writing, the more you practice, the more your skill grows.

Just Jobs or Challenging Careers?

Since you were little, people have been asking you, "What do you want to be when you grow up?" And your response has probably changed a zillion times over the years. A young girl's aspirations might change from ice skater to architect to lawyer to carpenter in the space of a week—depending on what TV shows she watched, what book she read, what guest speaker came to her classroom, or who won a gold medal at the Olympics. As a preteen, you still have lots of time to make a decision about the kind of work you want to do. But it's a good idea to start exploring careers now at a point in your life when you're figuring out who you really are, what kind of lifestyle suits you best, what hobbies appeal to you, and what subjects you're good at.

Changing Career Goals

Even when you're much older—in your twenties, perhaps—and you're already holding a job, your career goals might change. That's the great thing about the modern world of work—the always-present possibility of switching jobs to something more in line with your current interests and needs.

Liz Says:

From what I've seen with my brother, high school seems a lot harder than middle school. He spends more time on homework, and he even studies for tests once in a while! I know the high school he attends, which is the one I'll be going to, is bigger than my middle school. But I'm sure I'll be able to find my way around it just as he did.

Example: Sarah had always dreamed of becoming a dancer, but a serious injury prevented this dream from becoming a reality. She started to explore her new options and realized that she could still enjoy dance, but maybe more in a recreational way than as a professional in the field. Dreams also get adjusted when young women find out that the career they had in mind is different from what they had imagined or they realize that they just don't have the temperament or personality to hold that position.

Example: Jennifer's dream of being an elementary school teacher fizzled out after she started her student teaching as a college student. She quickly recognized that she didn't have the endless patience to deal with the constant demands of a room full of little kids five days a week. She also realized that her woodworking hobby that had gradually come to consume more of her free time could become more than a hobby. She decided to investigate carpentry or a related field as a possible career.

Liz Says:

I've wanted to have a million different careers since I was little. Everything from choreographer to actress to molecular biologist to film director to journalist. Right now, I don't have any particular career in mind, but I do want one that allows me to be creative and to help people. And there are lots of careers that will allow me to do that.

Jobs Versus Careers: What's the Difference?

Maybe you've heard some adults talk about their work as a job—sometimes even as "just a job"—while others have described what they do as careers. What's the difference? Plenty! A job is work that you do to get a paycheck, to fill your day, to be with other people. The tasks that you do in a job may hold some interest for you, but they're not the primary reason for working. Jobs are not likely to lead to more responsibility, more complex work, or significantly greater income as the years go by. If this description doesn't sound very attractive, start thinking now about careers, instead of jobs.

Here's a way to think about careers:

Challenging work that
Allows you to grow.
Responsibilities increase, and
Energy is high because it's work that
Excites you.
Retirement is something you can't imagine doing.

So what's the difference between a job and a career? Careers are fulfilling, enjoyable, challenging. They follow a path of increasing responsibility and new adventures. While a good income is important to almost everyone, people who hold careers work for far more than money. Years ago, few women held careers. Today, lots of women do. And their careers are in every field from medicine to sports to teaching to sales.

Do the quiz on page 188 to learn about what might be good for you. Remember, your answers give you some clues as to how you'd approach work now. Expect to change your mind many, many times as you grow up and even during your adult years. And that's good, because it means you don't have to stay with an occupation that bores you or a job where you're treated unfairly.

Trends in the Job Market

Although no one knows for sure which careers will be hot in the future, some government experts make predictions to help industries and people prepare for what's ahead. Not surprisingly, the occupations that are growing fastest

A Career Quiz

Answer these ten questions to learn a little about what kinds of environments and careers might appeal to you and what you might do to get ready for the world of work.

1. Would you rather work indoors or outdoors?

2. Which seems more attractive to you—working in a big office building with lots of people or in a small workplace with just a few employees?

3. Do you like being in charge, or would you prefer that someone else make the important decisions?

4. Would you rather work with adults, younger kids, animals, or machines?

5. Do you enjoy speaking or performing in front of groups, or would you prefer to work behind the scenes?

6. When you're very involved in a task, do you still notice your surroundings, or are you basically oblivious to your environment so you could be anywhere?

7. If you had to choose between a lot of travel or a lot of money, which would you want?

8. Would you like your work to have the same basic structure and schedule, or do you prefer work that involves new adventures and a different schedule each day?

9. Is it more important for you to help people or to influence them?

10. Do you like the challenge of learning about new technology, or are you intimidated by change, particularly when it involves strange machines?

What do your answers mean?

1. If you prefer working indoors, lots of careers would work for you, anything from teaching elementary school to managing a department in a large company. But if your preference is to spend time outdoors, you'll have to think a little harder about the range of careers open to you. Some possibilities are forest ranger, coach for a sport that is usually played outdoors, wildlife educator in a zoo, nature specialist, or camp director. What else can you come up with? Ask friends and family members, too.

2. If you think you'd like the noise and excitement of lots of people working in close quarters but have never really been in that kind of environment, try to get permission to spend some time in just that type of office. You might find the pace and occasional chaos attractive, or you might feel like holding your hands over your ears as you run as fast and as far away as you can from that workplace. Some personalities are better suited to cozy, intimate environments, while others thrive in a place that's jumping all the time. Experiment to see where you feel most comfortable.

3. Your answer to the question about being in charge could change every six months or so. Right now, you might feel more comfortable with someone else making the decisions. But as you get older and your self-confidence increases, you might actually enjoy the feeling of power you get from being in charge. Whether you're the type who's already showing signs of leadership ability or you know you'll need lots of support to become more of a leader, search out opportunities to develop those skills even further. Think of school, Girl Scouting, religious groups, community organizations, or after-school clubs as possible resources to gain that experience.

4. If you'd rather be with animals than humans, lots of jobs would make sense—veterinarian, kennel or horse ranch owner, or animal

(continues)

(continued from page 189)

trainer, for example. If your talents and temperament point you toward working with little kids, some possibilities are teacher, pediatrician, photographer (you have to understand kids to get great pictures of them), or child care worker. What if you have a knack for working with machines? Engineering or designing computer hardware might be in your future.

5. Lots of jobs require public speaking, some more than others. Politicians, teachers, corporate trainers, TV or radio reporters, and lawyers all use public speaking in their work. If making presentations doesn't scare you, great! But if it does, don't think you have to find a career that keeps you hidden. Instead, start working on becoming more comfortable in front of an audience. See the tips in chapter 2 and start practicing.

6. If you get so engrossed in your work that you forget where you are, you'd probably be happy in any work environment as long as the position interested you. But if your moods are affected by where you are, you'll have to take that into consideration when you start exploring career possibilities. Lots of people turn down jobs because an office is dark and dingy, and they'd rather not spend hours in that kind of unpleasant environment.

7. Choosing between travel and money is the kind of decision you might have to make one day. But if you're lucky—and smart—you might choose a field that offers both, if that's what you want. Have you ever considered international investment banking? Because so many careers today have an international component and because so many people in the United States speak languages other than English, becoming bilingual (if you don't already speak two languages) or even trilingual could be a real plus when it comes time to go into business or find a job. The earlier you start learning another language, the easier it will be for you to become fluent.

8. Some people like to know exactly what will happen each day, while others thrive on change and the unknown. Where do you fit? If you always follow the straight and narrow, maybe you'd like to see what would happen if you allowed your wild side to emerge—at least once in a while. Always being predictable can get very boring. But you have to know how much structure you need to feel comfortable. If you usually prefer clear boundaries, you might feel constantly on edge in a position where you could never predict what the next minute would bring.

9. Careers that involve helping other people range from physical therapist to socialworker. Many adults find tremendous satisfaction doing that kind of work. However, some girls grow up thinking that they should *always* be helping others. Not that there's anything wrong with being a caring person. But some girls carry this tendency too far. Taking care of everyone else's needs before thinking at all about herself can become unhealthy. Many women also shy away from work that involves influencing other people, perhaps because they haven't had the kind of experience that helps them feel comfortable exerting control over others. Just hearing the words *control* or *influence* makes them shake. However, many interesting careers, such as attorney, lobbyist, economist, and reporter, involve wielding influence. Why eliminate them from your range of future possibilities?

10. Whether you are extremely interested in computers and other technologies, use them occasionally, or avoid all contact with them, it's important to recognize that computers are a fact of life in the twenty-first century. It would be hard to imagine a career that doesn't involve the use of computers in one form or another. So whether you become an architect, a zoologist, or anything in between (that is, careers from A to Z), you'll be using computers in your work life. (See page 194 for more on computers.)

are computer related, with computer engineers at the top of the list. Other jobs in the computer field that are expected to flourish in coming years are systems analysts and desktop publishing specialists.

But there is a large gap between the number of women and men in these fields. While almost half of the total workforce in this country is female, women account for only about a quarter of the workers in technology jobs and even less in the top technology jobs. Growing fields that are not computer related include paralegals and legal assistants, medical and physician assistants, and social and human service assistants.

Which fields are going down in numbers? Child care workers in the home (but the number of child care workers in day care facilities is expected to increase), sewing machine operators, and farmers are among the occupations that are expected to show decreases.

What does all this mean to you? These predictions can help you think about what courses you might want to take or clubs you might want to join in high school. But remember that trends are just that—job predicting is not an exact science. World or national events or major discoveries or inventions could change the trends. So, while it's important to

Liz Says:

I've had the experience of working behind the scenes as well as appearing on stage in different musical revues. The first time, I was part of a technical crew of a camp show when I was ten. I could have performed, but at that time I was too shy. But in the last year or so, I've gotten more comfortable in front of audiences. Just a few weeks ago, I performed in the musical revue at my religious school. I had lots of fun and was much less nervous than I expected to be when it was time for my solo. And I guess I did pretty well since so many people complimented me on my performance. That made me feel really great.

know what's likely to happen down the road, you can't totally rely on these predictions because they will and do change. But they can offer helpful information, as long as you keep in mind that they're "best guesses" and not absolute truths. Also, if you have your heart set on a particular career, but it's not likely to be one of the hot jobs at the time that you're ready to find one, don't automatically eliminate that dream. Even fields that are slowing down have openings—they just may be harder to find. But since you will spend so much of your adult life working, you might as well do something you enjoy and are good at.

Talk to Working Women

If you want to get the real scoop on what it's like to have a particular occupation and what you need to do to be successful at it, get the information from someone who's already working in the field. Here are some questions you might ask:

Interview Guide

1. Why did you choose this particular field?

   _____

2. What kind of education or training is required for this job? What courses would be helpful but not necessarily required?

   _____

3. What do you like the most about this kind of work?

   _____

4. What do you like the least about your job?

   _____

5. If you could start all over again, would you still choose this career? Why or why not?

   _____

6. What advice can you give to someone my age who might enter your field?

   _____

Changing the Computer Culture

It's obvious that computers will continue to play a significant role in society. But did you know that research shows that girls and boys use computers in different ways? For example, more girls than boys go online, and when they use the Internet, they use it in different ways. Girls are more likely than boys to get homework help online, and girls also send more e-mail messages than boys. But boys and girls are about equal when it comes to receiving e-mail messages. Is that surprising to you? Girls, more than boys, see technology as a way to communicate and connect with others. Boys, on the other hand, are more likely to use the Internet to play games or to collect sports statistics

While girls and boys may be equally comfortable using computers, girls are far less likely to take the kind of high school and college computer courses that will provide them with the skills they need for high-level technology careers. Part of the reason for this is the "computer culture," which many girls see as masculine, intense, and competitive and not open to females. But if girls are going to enjoy the exciting job opportunities that require an understanding of sophisticated technology, they need to start preparing for them during their preteen and teen years. And they need to convince themselves that their style of using computers is just as good, just as valid as the boys' model. Maybe it's different from the way boys operate, but that doesn't make it inferior.

Famous Firsts

First female dentist with an official degree: Lucy B. Hobbs, 1866

First female airplane designer: Lillian Todd, 1906

First woman to fly alone across the Atlantic Ocean: Amelia Earhart, 1928

First Olympic athlete to score a perfect 10: Nadia Comaneci, 1976

First female United States Supreme Court Justice: Sandra Day O'Connor, 1981

How often do you use computers? Have you taken a course or thought about learning a computer language? Are you interested in designing a Web site? Do you understand how the hardware of computers works? Can you program a VCR? Set up a printer or scanner? Try taking some risks when you're using technology. Instead of immediately calling to your brother or dad when you run into trouble, experiment yourself to figure out the way to solve a computer problem.

How's this idea for a risk: If the computer club at school is all-male right now (and lots of them are), break the gender barrier. If you're really brave, go it alone. But if you need some support, and that's okay, get a friend or two to join you. And if no such club exists, be the girl who starts one. Find a female teacher or administrator with an interest in computers and a commitment to girls moving ahead in technology to work with you. When you do your part to change the computer culture, you're not only helping yourself, you're also doing a favor for loads of other girls out there.

Being an Entrepreneur

Do you like the idea of working for yourself rather than for a boss? Are you creative? Are you self-disciplined, or do you need someone practically standing over you all day to make sure you get your work done? Have you ever thought about being your own boss? You don't have to wait until you're older to be an entrepreneur—a person who starts her own business. Why not think about what you can do right now to become an entrepreneur? But how do you get started? These are the basic ingredients:

* An idea for a product or service that serves a need in your community (If no one wants what you're offering, you've got an uphill battle selling your product or service.)
* A plan for starting and growing your business (You can use the list on page 196.)

❀ Some money for supplies and publicity (perhaps flyers you can hand out at school)

❀ A place to conduct your business (Will you be using your basement as your workshop? Does a relative have space you can "rent"?)

❀ Some knowledge of how to run a business (for example, keeping track of expenses and income)

❀ A name for your business (This is more important than you might think. Businesses sometimes pay thousands of dollars to consultants to come up with a company name.)

Why would you even want to start a business? Because it will help you become more self-confident, give you experience making and managing money (more about that topic on page 198), allow you to make decisions, and provide you with opportunities to develop your leadership, organizational, and communication skills.

My Business Plan

What product or service will you be offering to customers?

_____

How is the product or service unique—different in some way from everything else out there?

_____

Who will your customers be?

_____

How will you attract customers to your business?

_____

What competition already exists for this product or service?

_____

How will you produce your product or service?

_____

What materials or people do you need to help you? Are they available?

_____

How will you raise the money to get started?

_____

How will you maintain your business as it goes along, particularly if your customers are not as interested in your product or service as you had hoped?

_____

Do This: To become more inspired about becoming an entrepreneur, find a woman who has her own business. Talk to her about the positives as well as the pitfalls in her work life. You don't have to be sure your business will be a success before you begin. If everyone needed to do that, no one would be in business. Hope (and work) for the best, but prepare for the worst. And if one business doesn't work out, but you're still interested in being an entrepreneur, analyze what went wrong. Figure out how to avoid those problems in the future. Review your business plan and see where your greatest challenges were.

6 6 6

Did you have a great product but not an effective way to market it? Did you offer a service that no one needed? Did you run out of money before your business had a chance to get off the ground? Answering these kinds of questions will help you make better decisions the next time around.

Liz Says:

When I was seven years old, my brother started a jewelry business with some friends. I was inspired by their actions to start my own business. I decided to use my newfound hobby of making miniatures and turn it into a business. After a while, my brother and his friends decided to give up their business, which was called "Just Jewelry." They sold the supplies and stock to me, which I combined with my business, which at that time was called "Caring and Sharing." I have no idea why I gave my business that name, but when I started my new company, I gave it the name of "Pins, Pearls, and Pendants." I sold my merchandise to family, friends, and people at my mom's office. Sometimes, I made up special orders for people who wanted an item to match a hobby or their clothing. Once I made a softball and glove pin for a woman who played the game. When I started concentrating on miniatures, rather than jewelry, I changed my business name to "Little Bits," which had been a nickname given to me by my nursery school teacher years ago because I was so small. The name Little Bits also sounds a little bit like my real name Elizabeth, so it's a fitting name for my company.

Money Talk

Do you know what else will prepare you to fulfill your dreams? Money. This is a good time for you to start learning how to handle it, save it, invest it, and spend it. Well, maybe spending it is not something you have to learn, but the rest of it would be valuable to know more about!

Years ago, many girls believed that they didn't have to learn about financial matters since they expected to marry men who would have stable jobs and adequate salaries. Today, most girls realize that becoming financially independent is an important goal. Even when women marry, one income in today's world is rarely enough to sustain a comfortable lifestyle, particularly when children are in the picture. Some women never marry, and others get divorced. Husbands lose jobs or become too disabled or ill to work; some die at a young age. In short, no one gets a guarantee that wishing for a financially secure future will make it so.

Consumer Savvy

Becoming a smart consumer is one way to be wise about money. Do this activity with a friend: Pretend you each have $500 to spend on clothing and entertainment for a month. You can actually go to stores with your "money" or search through catalogues to make your purchases. Here are some key questions for smart shoppers to think about:

* Do you compare prices at different stores?
* Do you recognize that sometimes the same basic item is priced differently depending on the label?
* Do you look for items that are marked down?
* Do you think about using coupons?
* Do you make realistic judgments about how much you really need or will use each item before you make a purchase?

Notice that need is not the only criterion you should use. Getting something just because you will wear and enjoy it is not a bad way to make decisions—but only if the item is within your budget. However, if you really need a winter jacket but instead spend your money on an extravagant party dress that you fell in love with but don't really have an occasion for wearing, you know that's not being money-smart.

Decide also on the kind and amount of entertainment you will spend your money on. Maybe you'll learn that if you go to the movies on certain days or at certain times, you'll save on the ticket price. Perhaps your newspaper carries coupons that you can use for the game arcade that you visit. You and a friend might decide to rent a video, splitting the cost, instead of buying tickets for a movie. When it comes to spending money, there are always lots of options.

List in table 8-1 what you bought, and ask your friend to do the same.

By reviewing your filled-in chart, you'll be able to see how many of your decisions were well thought out. Compare your purchases with those made by your friend, and then discuss how you each made choices. Did your friend use a strategy that you might try when shopping in the future? Maybe you can share an effective technique that you used. That way, you'll both benefit, and that's important when you have real money to spend. Shopping with pretend money is a painless way to learn money management.

Saving and Investing

Smart shopping is only one way to manage money. Saving and investing are also important tools on your path to financial independence. When you put money in the bank, you might receive interest, which is an amount the bank gives you in exchange for allowing it to use your money. Of course, you get it

Table 8-1. Smart Buying

	Cost	Good Decision?
Item You Bought		❑ Yes ❑ No
Item You Looked at but Didn't Buy		❑ Yes ❑ No

back when you want it, and even if the bank fails (that happens, but very rarely), the government usually guarantees that you'll still get your money. Saving money in the bank is a safe way to increase its worth, but it grows very slowly.

Investing in stocks and mutual funds is another strategy. *Stocks* are very tiny pieces of individual companies. What's your favorite athletic shoe manufacturer? What brand of breakfast cereal do you eat most often? If these companies are publicly traded, you could own shares in them. In general, as a company becomes more successful, the price increases. So if you buy five shares at $10 each, and the stock price goes up to $15, you've made $25. Sounds easy, doesn't it? But it's not. Stock prices rise and fall for lots of different reasons. Some make sense, but others don't. Experts use all kinds of fancy formulas to try to predict the direction of stock prices, and some do better than others, but they're still guessing. Why not see how you compare to the experts? Choose ten stocks and follow them for one month. Then see what would have happened if you had actually bought them. And try to learn what world, national, or company events influenced the price changes.

Some people invest in mutual funds instead of in individual stocks. When you invest in a mutual fund, you are buying into many different companies that have been selected by experts. That way, if one business loses a lot of money, maybe even goes bankrupt, the other companies in the fund can balance out the loss. Of course, if one company in the fund is enormously successful, maybe tripling its worth in a short time, you might not see very much change since your mutual fund is made up of many different companies, and that big gain gets averaged into all the other gains and losses.

Getting an Allowance

Do you receive an allowance from your parents? Many kids do, but some don't. Giving allowance to kids is a decision parents make, sometimes with input from their children. If you don't already receive an allowance, you might want

Liz Says:

I have been getting an allowance since I was about six years old. At that time, I received just $0.50 a week, but I didn't have to buy anything with it. Each year on my birthday, until I was nine, my allowance increased by $0.75. When I was nine, my parents raised my allowance significantly since I was able to understand at that point how to manage it. When I was ten, I opened a savings account, and whenever I have about $60 or more at home, I add that to the bank account. Only once did I take any money out, and that was to buy a few shares of a stock, which has gone down in value. It's starting to go back up now, but it's still below the price I paid. I also contribute 10 percent of my allowance to our family vacation fund. Occasionally, I contribute some money to charity as well. I like being able to make decisions about my money.

to mention to your parents that figuring out what to do with your allowance is one of the best ways to learn how to manage money. Keep track of where your allowance goes, so you'll be able to detect patterns of spending and saving.

One of the big questions girls your age ask is "How much allowance should I be getting?" Notice that this is a different question from "How much allowance do I need?" or "How much allowance do I want?" And the answer may not be the one you're looking for. It all depends. On where you live—some places are much more expensive than others. On what you're expected to buy with it—will you need to use your allowance for school lunches or transportation costs? On how much you're supposed to put aside for savings. On how much you are expected to donate to a charity or a special family fund. On whether you'll be buying gifts for friends and family members with the money.

Some of your allowance should be discretionary—that is, it's up to you to decide how to use it. If you get a regular allowance, you might want to set a savings goal. Then you put aside a portion of your allowance each week until you have saved enough to buy something that's pretty expensive like a CD. Or you might choose to spend the discretionary money each week or so to purchase small, inexpensive items like gum or a magazine. It's all up to you.

Managing Stress

Big dreams often translate into big stress. If one of your goals is to make the varsity swimming team, you may need to set your alarm for 5 A.M. to get your practice in before classes start. If you want to do well in school, you'll have to put extra effort into your English project instead of just slapping together any old thing. If you want to buy a CD player, you may have to do a lot of tutoring or dog walking or lawn mowing to collect enough funds.

With your life already full of homework, chores, projects, sports practices, music lessons, and whatever else is crammed into it, you may feel as if adding one more thing will push you over the edge. But then, you find out about an opportunity that's just too good to pass up—a chance to hear the hottest group perform on the Sunday before a major school project is due. Or maybe the temptation is the offer of free tickets to a baseball game—with seats right behind your team's dugout—but they're for the night you put aside for finally getting to the studying you postponed all week.

Maybe stress is not the first thought that pops into your head when these once-in-a-lifetime opportunities come your way. But even the most positive experience is sometimes stress inducing if it means making a tough choice or having to work harder than usual. And then there's always the stress that comes from any negative event, from a fight with your best friend to losing your allowance after it slipped unnoticed through a hole in your pocket.

Learning to manage stress effectively is a vital skill for your mental and physical well-being. Here are some tips for you to try when life seems overwhelming to you:

❧ Write in your journal. Often, just expressing how you feel will provide you with some relief. And many girls find that when they write about a problem, they actually begin to figure out a way to deal with it.

❧ Go outdoors (unless it's 20 below zero Fahrenheit or 100 degrees in the shade) and walk briskly or jog for at least twenty minutes. Hopping, skipping, or jumping would work, too, but you might feel foolish, adding to your stress!

❧ Read a book or magazine that's not required for school. Try something that's light and fun, or maybe get involved in a complex mystery to get your mind off your problems.

❧ Call, write a letter, or e-mail a friend. Sometimes misery loves company. Tell your friend whether you want advice or just someone to listen to you.

❧ Add bath salts or bubbles to a warm bath, and cleanse your mind of everything but the sensations of your bath—the wonderful aroma and the soothing temperature.

Liz Says:

Some of the time when I feel stressed, I turn on music and dance. At other times, I like to read. It calms me down because I get so involved in the story that it's like I'm in another world and don't think any more about my own problems.

❧ Do some simple yoga moves or meditate for at least ten minutes or until you can feel your muscles relaxing and stress leaving your body.

❧ Talk to a parent or another trusted adult who can help you decide on actions you can take to reduce the tension you're experiencing. Maybe you're involved in too many activities and need to cut out one or more of them. Just because you enjoy lots of activities and are talented in many areas doesn't mean that you have to be caught up in all of them simultaneously. If this is your issue, give yourself a break—slow down.

Dreams are a powerful part of life. They drive you forward, yet they can carry you to a place of complete relaxation. Dreaming about the future will help you prepare for it—you'll explore careers and learn about managing money. But be careful that you don't live so much in the future that you forget about enjoying and living in the moment. Think about what you experienced today. Did you just rush through preparing for tomorrow? Or did you find some time to appreciate the sounds and smells, questions and laughter that together made up your life today?

Some Final Words

Harriet says: This book has taken you—and us—through a lot of topics, everything from seeing how unique you are to making hard decisions about smoking and drinking, from starting your own business or community service project to finally dreaming about your future.

Have you learned more about yourself as a result of the quizzes and charts you've completed? I hope you had fun with them, maybe even some good laughs, and that you gained new insights into who you are and where you think you're going in life.

Each chapter contains lots of facts and many different ideas. Perhaps even more important are the hundreds of questions the book raises. That's why I'd like you to think about this book as one that doesn't really have an ending. Even if you had read every single word and worked on every last activity (wow, that would be an incredible accomplishment), I'd want you to continue using this book. As issues come up in your life, use this book as your personal assistant. Allow it to help you make positive decisions right now as well as prepare you for the challenges that lie ahead.

Liz Says: As I worked on this book, including completing many of the quizzes, I found out a lot about myself. Perhaps most important, I learned that my mom and I could work together on a big project, that I can actually write, and that I enjoy expressing myself.

I hope that you've learned a great deal about yourself and about your life and that you'll use some of the advice in your everyday life. I know that I'll be using some of it as I finish up my preteen years and go on to being a real teenager.

Lastly, I'd like to answer the question that's the title of this book: What's so bad about being good? Although my mom and I took more than 200 pages to write about it, the simple answer is: nothing—nothing at all!

About the Authors

*H*arriet S. Mosatche, Ph.D., is the director of program development for Girl Scouts of the U.S.A. In that position, she writes or directs the writing of resources for girls from five to seventeen and for the adults who work with them. Since 1997, Harriet and her daughter, Liz, have offered advice in "Ask Dr. M," a popular section of the "Just 4 Girls" pages (www.girlscouts.org /girls) of the national Girl Scouts Web site.

In addition to her work with Girl Scouts, Harriet is a partner in OutPerform LLC, which offers consulting services to schools and community agencies in program development and evaluation. She also conducts workshops on child and adolescent development and family relationships for parents, kids, and teachers.

Harriet received her Ph.D. in developmental psychology from the City University of New York. Prior to joining the Girl Scouts organization, she was a college professor for a dozen years, with six of those years as chairperson of the Psychology Department at a New York City college.

Her publications include articles in scholarly journals and popular magazines as well as two books, the most recent being *Too Old for This, Too Young for That! Your Survival Guide for the Middle-School Years* (coauthored with Karen Unger), a 2000 Gold Award winner for nonfiction from the National Association of Parenting Publications.

Harriet has volunteered as a Girl Scout leader since 1993 and now works with a troop of twelve- and thirteen-year-old Cadette Girl Scouts. She lives in New York with her husband, Ivan Lawner, and their two children, Rob and Liz.

Elizabeth (Liz) K. Lawner is a seventh-grader who has been offering advice to girls around the world since she was in the fourth grade. With her mom, Liz writes answers on the "Ask Dr. M" section of the Just 4 Girls pages of the national Girl Scouts Web site. Although she has enjoyed writing for many years, this is the first time she has contributed to a book.

Liz has her own business, Little Bits, selling her handmade miniatures and jewelry. She has studied dance—hip hop, jazz, and tap—since she was four and enjoys playing piano. Liz is also a talented student and received the highest score in her school on the American Mathematics Competition in 2000.

Liz has been active in Girl Scouting since she was five years old and is now a Cadette Girl Scout. She lives in New York with her parents and brother, Rob.

Index

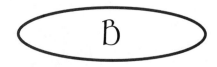

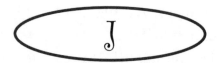
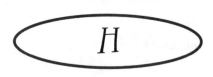
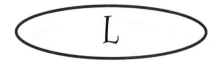

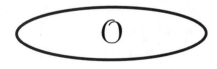

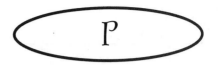

A Teen's Guide to the Best Place on Earth

Want to have a great time at Disney World—beyond the typical kid's stuff? This is the first book to give you insider tips on the hottest parks and rides. From MGM's Tower of Terror to water rides at Universal's Islands of Adventure that will leave you dripping, you'll get a teen's perspective on what's hot (and what's not), including:

- **The coolest—and scariest—rides**
- **How not to get trapped in a lame show**
- **Music, shows, and popular hot spots for teens**
- **And much more!**

Also included is information on Epcot Center, MGM Studios, Animal Kingdom, Universal Studios, and the Islands of Adventure.

ISBN 0-7615-2627-7 / Paperback / 192 pages
U.S. $12.95 / Can. $19.95

THREE RIVERS PRESS

Available everywhere books are sold.
Visit us online at www.crownpublishing.com.